Blackjack

A Winner's Handbook

Other books by Jerry L. Patterson:

CASINO GAMBLING
(with Eric Nielsen and "Sharpshooter")

BREAK THE DEALER
(with Eddie Olsen)

BLACKJACK'S WINNING FORMULA

SPORTS BETTING
(with Jack Painter)

Blackjack

A Winner's Handbook

JERRY L. PATTERSON
with Eric Nielsen

A Perigee Book

A Perigee Book
Published by The Berkley Publishing Group
A division of Penguin Putnam Inc.
375 Hudson Street
New York, New York 10014

First edition: July 2001
Published simultaneously in Canada.

The Penguin Putnam Inc. World Wide Web site address is
www.penguinputnam.com

Library of Congress Cataloging-in-Publication Data

Patterson, Jerry L.
Blackjack, a winner's handbook / Jerry L. Patterson.—Rev. and updated.
p.   cm.
ISBN 0-399-52683-8
1. Blackjack (Game)   I. Title: Winner's handbook.   II. Title.
GV1295.B55 P37   2000
795.4'23—dc21   00-051042

Printed in the United States of America

10 9 8 7 6 5 4 3 2 1

This one is for my blackjack instructors without whose support I could not have pulled off this final update of *Blackjack: A Winner's Handbook*:

Donnie (007) Bond: Give him a system to learn and he shakes it right down to its foundations, becoming an expert and a teacher in the same amount of time that most gamblers would have barely tiptoed into the water.

Robert (Blackjack Bob) Bowser, whose intense analytical mind and powers of observation allow him to see the game of blackjack from another dimension, finding winning clues that few others would ever see.

Robin (High Five) Frost, whose unique combination of friendship, enthusiasm, humor, and wisdom contributed greatly to my motivation for undertaking and completing this final update.

Harry (Hammer) Gay, who asked me to teach him all that I know about blackjack and then garnered this knowledge by working with me and my instructors to develop an excellent advanced blackjack course and, in the doing, became a top-notch blackjack instructor himself.

Darcy (Dr. Stats) Hanson, who has a way with analysis and numbers that penetrate the veil of today's blackjack game, disclosing winning insights that are extremely useful in our Blackjack Masters training program.

John (Warhorse) Higdon, who has been with me longer than the others, is a fixture in our follow-up training program and whom neither I, nor my students, could do without.

Bill (Killer) Konrad who knows, more than anyone, when to play and when not to play. When he plays, more often than not, he will walk away a winner for the session. His insights on betting and money management have been vital to the success of hundreds of our students.

Eric (Guardian) Nielsen, a true guardian of our little gaming empire, who never saw a casino game for which he couldn't analyze and devise a method for overcoming the house edge, thus delivering an advantage to his friends and JPE clients.

And for Sharpshooter, who would score at the blackjack table if he ever finds the time to turn his attention from craps and roulette to cards.

Contents

SECTION FOUR
THE INTERNET—PITFALLS AND POSSIBILITIES

SECTION FIVE
PRODUCTS AND SERVICES AVAILABLE FROM JERRY PATTERSON

ABOUT THE AUTHOR

HOME STUDY COURSES

ACKNOWLEDGMENTS

My Internet friends—Jerry Garner, Ted Loh, and many others too numerous to mention—for sharing with me their insights on Internet casinos, blackjack web sites, and their knowledge of how to choose an honest and fair Internet casino for play.

Judy ("Fletch") Fletcher for always being there when I needed her, for running my little gaming outfit efficiently and productively, thus freeing me up for the time to devote to this final update, for delivering the highest level of customer service in JPE's quarter-century history to our many hundreds of clients, and for being one of the finest people I have ever known and will ever have the privilege of knowing.

And to Michael Lutfy, my editor at Perigee Books, whose creative editing and insight into the book's contents was crucial in inspiring me to do the very best that I could do in producing this last revision of *Blackjack: A Winner's Handbook*.

WHAT THE REVISED EDITION OF *BLACKJACK: A WINNER'S HANDBOOK* WILL DO FOR YOU:

- Explain the changes in the game and show you how you can profit from them.
- Show you how to choose an honest and fair Internet casino for play.
- Enable you to get an edge at Internet casinos before your first hand is dealt.
- Show you how to cull usable information from the thousands of blackjack web sites on the Internet.
- Reveal new information about the automatic shuffling machines, both the two-shoe type and the continuous shufflers, including a proven winning system.
- Disclose that card counting does not always work and describe what you can do to avoid losing.
- Describe Count Profiles: a bold new strategy for beating the shoe game.
- Teach you how to play the game (if you are a beginning player) and show you a simple basic strategy for playing each and every blackjack hand to maximize your gain and minimize your loss.
- Show you how to manage your gambling money so you're always in control, whether you're a beginner or an advanced player.

- Provide a five-step strategy for learning how to develop and use mental discipline to avoid losing and to increase your winning edge.
- Explain table biases caused by the casinos' nonrandom shuffle, how to avoid the dealer biases, and how to turn the player biases to your advantage.
- Provide you with a four-phased strategy, called Takedown, which minimizes losses while enabling you to score in those games where the dealer is breaking and the players are winning.
- Give you a complete home-practice program, including learning drills, for basic strategy players and card counters.
- Tell you stories of team blackjack and teach you how to use team-play techniques to multiply your profits.
- Introduce a seven-step, winning program that will assist you to effectively utilize all of the powerful data in this book.
- Reveal extremely useful data for those blackjack players considering playing the game to make a living: a four-stage plan for becoming a professional blackjack player.
- Show you how to contact the author and join a network of blackjack winners!

One

INTRODUCTION AND OVERVIEW

INTRODUCTION

This book has been in print since 1977, through three major editions, and longer than all but two other blackjack books.

Why, then, a new, fourth edition?

The explosion of casino gambling locations is the first of five reasons that prompted this new edition. When the 1990s edition of this book was published, just two states offered blackjack games; now you can belly up to a blackjack table in over twenty states.

But these "land-based" casinos are only part of the story. If you total up all the casinos across America offering casino blackjack, your number would be less than half of the casinos residing in a new medium alone—the Internet. You can visit over eight hundred casinos in this new medium without leaving your home—by dialing up their web sites on your computer. Thus, the second reason for this update: to address the proliferating Internet casinos.

The third reason for revising this book also concerns the Internet: a plethora of gambling and blackjack-related web sites that offer blackjack information. Such web sites will be discussed in detail to assist both the wary and unwary blackjack player to evaluate this vast amount of available data.

The primary goal of this book throughout its various editions has always been to teach you how to win in today's blackjack environment. To accomplish this goal, four winning strategies were published in the 1990s edition. Three involved card counting and incorporated the advantages of playing table biases (explained later in this book), and one was a noncounting system. Reader feedback rated these systems very highly, but, unfortunately, casino countermeasures have made the card counting systems all but obsolete. Don't get me wrong. You can still win by counting cards. But only if you have the skill and discipline of counting down a six- or eight-deck shoe, have the patience to wait for the long term, or if you understand how to apply card counting to clump-card games (which you will learn in this new edition). Traditional card counting works very well in single-and double-deck games such as those found in Las Vegas, in northern Nevada, and in a few other locations.

Casino countermeasures extend to more than barring midshoe entry. Automatic shuffling machines are now commonplace in many casinos. These machines are intended not only to speed up the game, but also to eliminate the advantage enjoyed by card counters and shuffle-trackers.

The randomized game they purportedly produce and the random-number-generated game offered by Internet casinos offered a compelling fourth reason for this revised edition: to assess the evolution of blackjack systems and methods for exploiting these new blackjack environments, and for exploiting changes in how casino management protects the game from exploitation by advantage players.

In the 1990s edition we assessed the impact of the increased number of decks coupled with the new shuffles on the traditional card counters' chances of winning. In our discussion of the evolution of blackjack systems and methods, we further assess this impact in some detail, and examine how card clumping has just about nullified the traditional card counters' chances of winning in the multi-deck shoe games. We offer hope to this beleaguered group with an innovative new card-counting system called Count Profiles.

There is a fifth and final reason for this new edition: the variations to traditional blackjack games, such as Spanish 21, which are now offered by many casinos. Are these games beatable? Should you spend your time playing them as opposed to sticking with the traditional games? These questions will be answered herein for the most popular of these blackjack variations.

BLACKJACK: SHORT-TERM VS. LONG-TERM PERSPECTIVES

Up until the publication of the major revision of my book, *Casino Gambling*, the casinos had a mathematical advantage in all the games of chance except blackjack. Blackjack has been considered a game of skill since the publication of Ed Thorp's *Beat the Dealer in 1961*. This skill, traditionally called card counting, gives the astute player a long-term advantage over the casino.

But how long is the long-term period of play? Players, mathematicians, and computer scientists have been pondering this question for many years without coming up with a satisfactory answer.

To me, however, long-term play is longer than the average playing session or even the average trip of any casino gambler or blackjack player. For instance, most blackjack players visit Atlantic City for an evening, a day, or a weekend. In Las Vegas, a weekend is the usual duration. These playing session durations have absolutely nothing to do with long-term mathematics.

In this book I will use *long-term* to refer to traditional card counters, those players who are prepared to commit several hundred playing hours, under the proper playing conditions, to achieve a mathematical advantage over the casino. But I will focus on short-term play, since this refers to the amount of time the majority of blackjack players devote to the game. The short term is what is happening right now, in this casino, at this blackjack table. In this book, you will learn to recognize short-term opportunities and how to exploit them.

You will learn that playing a short-term strategy is different from playing a long-term strategy. For instance, if you have been playing blackjack for any length of time, you have learned traditional blackjack techniques that are accepted today as axioms, such as basic strategy and card counting. This book takes a close look at these and other accepted blackjack traditions and departs from them for the benefit of the short-term player in the areas of stop-losses and stop-wins and up-as-you-lose betting strategies.

TRADITIONAL PLAYER VS. TODAY'S PLAYER

There are two terms used in this book that relate to what has been said above: *traditional player* (or traditional card counter) and *today's player*.

A *traditional player* is a person who uses a card-counting point-count system as his only winning tool and plays for the long run. He or she is not concerned with short-run fluctuations that may be due to table biases caused by the nonrandom shuffle. (These situations are described fully in later chapters.)

The term *new-era player* (also called *today's player*) is used to define the player who understands that the game has changed and who is open to considering new winning strategies and tactics oriented to both card counting and non–card counting strategies. *Today's player* understands the advantages of recognizing and exploiting short-term opportunities.

It is my hope in writing this book that you will become a *today's player*.

I ask you to read this book with an open mind. If you are skeptical, set aside some time on your next casino visit for some observations. Select one or two ideas from this book and observe them in the real world of casino-played blackjack. You will find, without risking a dime, that they really do work!

AN OVERVIEW OF THE BOOK

The information in this book is presented as five Sections.

Section One is The Foundation of Winning Play. Chapter 2 starts with the rules of play for casino blackjack, and should be read by all players not familiar with how the game is played.

Chapter 3 describes the basic strategy of blackjack, the origins of which go back to 1958, when four engineers worked out the superior play of each player-hand possibility against each dealer upcard possibility. The basic strategy has been refined and improved over the years with improved, state-of-the art computational techniques and has long been recognized as the first step on the player's road to becoming a winner. This chapter also includes memory aids for learning basic strategy and a complete handbook of basic strategy drills to facilitate the learning process. Do these drills, learn basic strategy cold, and then you can focus on one or more of several winning techniques described in subsequent chapters.

The Foundation of Winning Play also requires that you learn how to create and manage a blackjack bankroll, which is covered in Chapter 4. The one factor contributing most to player losses does not involve using the wrong system or bad luck, it involves a breakdown of mental discipline. If you follow the easy-to-use strategy for developing and executing mental discipline described in Chapter 5, you will have taken a giant step on your path to becoming a consistent winning player.

Chapter 6 shows you three variations to traditional blackjack games: Spanish 21, Multiaction blackjack, and No hole card blackjack. These variations will be compared to the traditional game.

Section Two documents the evolution of casino blackjack systems and methods. Card counting pros and cons are covered in Chapter 7, including dealing with the controversy over whether or not card counting still works in the shoe game. The status of advanced black-jack methods that are still viable is assessed in Chapters 8 and 9: Team Play and the Shuffle-tracking.

The reader is introduced in Chapter 10 to biases caused by the nonrandom shuffle, why they occur, and how they can be exploited, along with other winning innovations. Conclusions and recommen-dations for today's player are presented in Chapter 11 and are in-tended to lay the groundwork for the description of winning strategies presented in Sections Three and Four.

To support our overall assessment of the evolution of blackjack systems and methods, thirteen classic blackjack books are reviewed in Chapter 12. The inclusion of this list is intended to solve the problems of many newer players in confronting and selecting from the nearly two hundred blackjack books now in publication, and also to recognize those books that are timeless in the data and stories they contain.

Section Three describes winning blackjack systems for today's player in two categories: (1) two noncount strategies, including one for playing against the automatic shuffling machine; and (2) card counting systems that reflect the realities of card clumping in today's blackjack shoe games.

Chapter 13 describes Takedown, the very popular strategy intro-duced in the 1990s edition. It exploits table biases and is unique to this book. It is based on my close-to-fifty years of blackjack play, blackjack research, and blackjack instruction. It is a complete de-parture from traditional blackjack card counting because card count-ing, as discussed in this book, presents serious problems to most players for beating the shoe game. Chapter 13 concludes with changes to basic strategy that reflect the realities of like-card clump-ing. Even if you're a traditional card counter, but somewhat risk averse, consider adding these changes to your game plan.

Chapter 14 presents a proven strategy for playing against the automatic shuffle machines, one which exploits the unique profile that the randomly shuffled deck(s) engenders in this game.

Before getting to the card-counting methods described in Chapter 16, I arm the reader with a handbook of card-counting drills in Chapter 15. Even longtime traditional card counters will find these drills quite useful in keeping their game sharp. The card-counting method described in Chapter 16—Count Profiles—recognizes that like-card clumping distorts the information contained in the traditional point count and takes a totally new direction vis-à-vis winning blackjack methodologies presenting simple, intermediate, and advanced winning strategies.

The single-deck strategy presented in the 1990s edition is modified for the expanding number of two-deck games found in many casino locations, including Las Vegas. The reader will find this method, High-Low Plus, in Chapter 17.

One of the often-asked questions from blackjack players is covered in Chapter 18—How to Become a Professional Blackjack Player. The realities of this sometimes unrealistic goal are addressed with no punches pulled.

Section Four is all about the Internet and its impact on casino blackjack.

Chapter 19 describes the types of blackjack information available on the Internet, and the problems in assessing and using it. If you are surfing the Net and participating in blackjack chat rooms, posting to blackjack newsgroups and /or visiting blackjack web sites, you will find much in this chapter to interest you. And, if not, read it anyway because, sooner or later, you will be.

Chapter 20 tackles the issues surrounding Internet casinos including honesty, fairness, and the safety of sending money into cyberspace. The key decision of choosing one at which to play is addressed in detail.

Chapter 21 presents winning strategies, which are keyed to the unique characteristics of Internet casinos. Two strategies are presented, one exploiting Internet casino marketing strategies, and the other a method to beat the choppy games caused by the random-number-generator computer software all Internet casinos use to generate the blackjack hands.

Chapter 22 puts everything together with a seven-step winning program for all players — long term, short term, card counter and noncounter.

Section Five details the instructional programs offered by the author and his staff not only in blackjack, but also in two other games where the player can actually gain a statistical edge over the casino — in craps with a controlled throw, and in roulette by identifying dealer signatures that make the game predictable.

Your learning curve and your blackjack skills will advance rapidly as you read, study, and apply the data in this book. If you follow the principles documented herein, you will indeed be able to do what few gamblers do — take the casinos' money instead of losing yours to them.

HOW TO USE THIS BOOK

This book is intended for use by beginning, recreational, and experienced/advanced blackjack players.

If you are a beginner, start with Section One and learn the fundamentals. Basic strategy for playing the hands is mandatory. Just taking this first step will put you ahead of 90 percent of all blackjack players.

Players of all experience levels should also read and study Chapters 4 and 5 — about bankroll management and mental discipline. My experience in over twenty years of teaching the game is that most players are looking for a system as their panacea to winning, while these most important and crucial factors, occurring earlier in the learning curve, are often overlooked. So take some time to learn bankroll fundamentals, establish your bankroll, and then develop a game plan based on that bankroll. I guarantee it will pay off many times over in avoiding unnecessary losses and positioning you on the winning pathway.

If you bought this book looking for winning methods, you will find them in Sections Three and Four, but please do not overlook Section Two before you turn to the system description chapters. It is important for you to understand the baseline of blackjack systems and methods development, especially over the ten years leading up to the new millennium as casino locations expanded so rapidly and the Internet introduced a totally new dimension into the game. So reading and studying Chapters 7 through 18 of Sections Two and Three will give you the wherewithal to decide on which pathway you wish to choose, traditional or alternative, to achieve your goal of becoming a winning player and prepare you to decide upon which systems you wish to employ to get there.

If you have a computer and are on the Internet, Section Four, Chapters 19 and 20, are must-reads, even if you have no plans to play blackjack at an online casino or visit a blackjack web site. Internet casinos and blackjack web sites are all over the Net. Sooner or later you will run into one and the descriptive information in these three chapters will be extremely helpful in your first encounter and subsequently. If you do find yourself playing at an online casino, why not start the game with an edge? You will have an advantage right off the top by learning and using the winning method for Internet casinos explained in Chapter 21.

Read on and reap!

Section One

The Foundation of Winning Play

Two

BLACKJACK BASICS

HISTORY

Gambling with playing cards spread steadily throughout Europe after Johann Gutenberg printed the first deck in Germany in 1440, and many of the games involved drawing cards to reach a certain total. Although the exact relationship remains obscure, blackjack is believed to have evolved from several of these early games. Baccarat, with the magic number of nine, appeared in Italy about 1490, followed by the game of seven and a half, which seems to be the first game where the player automatically lost if he went over the desired number. The game of one and thirty was first played sometime before 1570 in Spain, and the duke of Wellington, the marquess of Queensbury, and Prime Minister Disraeli all played quince (fifteen) in Crockford's, the famous English casino, which flourished between 1827 and 1844. From France came *trente et quarante* (thirty and forty) and finally *vingt un* or *vingt et un* twenty-one or (twenty and one), which crossed the Atlantic ocean and was listed in the American Hoyle of 1875.

As first played in the United States, blackjack was a private game, but by the early 1900s, tables for twenty-one were being offered in

the gambling parlors of Evansville, Indiana. Acceptance was slow, and, to stimulate interest, operators offered to pay three to two for any count of twenty-one in the first two cards, and ten to one if the twenty-one consisted of the ace of spades and either the jack of spades or the jack of clubs. This hand was called, of course, blackjack. The ten-to-one payoff was soon eliminated, but the term remained, first as the name of any two-card twenty-one hand and subsequently as the name of the game itself, although twenty-one would have been more appropriate.

By 1919, tables covered with green felt and emblazoned in gold letters announcing "Blackjack Pays Odds of 3 to 2" were being manufactured in Chicago and appeared in illegal gambling halls throughout the country. The popularity of the game grew slowly until gambling was legalized in Nevada in 1931, then blackjack became the third most successful game, outstripping faro, but trailing both roulette and craps. Because of the prohibitive casino edge of 5.26 percent in roulette, discouraged players drifted away from the game, and by 1948 blackjack had become the second-biggest casino moneymaker.

TODAY'S GAME

In 1956, a book called *Playing Blackjack to Win* was written by Baldwin, Cantey, Maisel, and McDermott containing a nearly perfect basic strategy. This was followed in 1962 by Edward Thorp's book, *Beat the Dealer*, which refined the strategy and added a counting system. Now, for the first time, the sophisticated gambler could learn to play nearly even with the house, and perhaps with a slight edge in his favor. This scientifically developed information sparked a nationwide interest in blackjack that made it the number-one table game in American casinos throughout the 60s, 70s and into the 80s.

Because the table is less than half the size of those required for craps, roulette, or baccarat, with a corresponding reduction in both the number of players and casino personnel, blackjack is far less intimidating to the beginning player. Couple this with the simplicity of the basic rules — both the player and the dealer draw cards, and whoever comes closest to twenty-one without going over, wins — and you can understand the popularity of the game.

Blackjack is unique among the casino games in that any player can make decisions that will affect the results of the game. In addition, it is the only game where the outcome of one hand influences the following hands. Since the type of cards that have been played determines the value of the cards remaining to be played, the probability of winning or losing is in a constant state of flux, and although chance is still a significant factor, the skillful player enjoys a marked advantage over the novice. Obviously, the casinos are profit-making institutions, so why do they continue to offer a game where the player has a fair chance? Elementary, my dear reader, because over 90 percent of all players do not make a sufficient effort to learn the fundamentals of the game. Ironically, the fact that the game can be beaten is well known to the casino operators, but since very few players will be bothered to invest the necessary time to learn to play at this level, blackjack and its variations have become the most profitable table games in the house.

BLACKJACK BASICS

New casinos are still being designed and built in Nevada, Atlantic City, and other casino locations across the country, and hundreds of new casino gamers are trying their luck every day. Many of these neophytes know little or nothing about how to play or how to bet. To accommodate these newcomers, as well as the multitude of existing players who are not playing to their best advantage, let's thoroughly explore the basic elements of the game.

First of all, although you will find seven betting spots on the table, blackjack is not a group game. Each bettor is playing against the dealer and betting against the house; the number of players or where they sit has no effect on the ultimate outcome. Second, the decision to draw or not draw by any one player has no long-run effect on other players. Of course, in any one hand, the player to the right of you or the dealer appears to have significant control of the results of your hand, but really, the draw of each player at the table has an equal effect on the hand. Nevertheless, many players critically observe the play of the hand preceding the dealer, commonly called *third base*, with the result that most beginners shun this chair to avoid contention. Ninety percent of the bettors are there to enjoy themselves, and because of the game's frequent pauses for shuffling, dealing, and settling bets, you'll find an air of relaxation not always found at the other games. So if you happen to sit where there are disagreeable players, move to another table. Tables are almost always plentiful.

Chips

As soon as you sit down, you'll need chips. Place some currency alongside the betting circle directly in front of you; the dealer will announce the amount to the pit supervisor and exchange it for distinctly decorated clay disks, setting them in front of you as he pushes your money through the slot in the table into the concealed drop box. All the tables carry $1, $5, and $25 chips, frequently colored white, red, and green, and some tables keep $100 chips, usually black. The dealer's rack also contains half-dollars, but these are used only for settling odd bets such as the three to two payoff for a blackjack on a $3 or $5 wager. If you want to change a large-denomination chip for smaller ones, place it alongside your betting spot and announce, "Change, please." Never place it in the circle as it may be mistaken for a bet.

Although state regulations in most gambling locations prohibit the betting of cash, money wagers may be made in Nevada even though casinos there prefer the use of chips. Skillful dealers can add up the value of a stack of mixed chips in an instant because of the various colors; however all currency is green and the bills must be checked and rechecked. Casinos also realize that many bettors subconsciously do not place the same value on chips that they do on actual cash. Somehow, many people feel that once they give up their money for chips, it's not really their's anymore; subsequently, players find it infinitely easier to push out four green chips than to reach into their wallets and extract $100 bills.

Most gaming locations have regulations that prohibit the using of chips from one casino in different casino. This practice used to be prevalent in Nevada. However, because junketeers, who were required to buy in for a certain sum in order to qualify for complimentary rooms, meals, and travel, frequently reneged on their obligation to play at the tables by converting their chips to cash in other casinos, the interchange of chips between casinos has just about become a thing of the past. So be sure to cash in your chips at the casino cashier before departing the casino.

As you stack your chips, you may notice one or two small signs displayed near the dealer. One often lists the casino's particular blackjack rules, and the other indicates the minimum and maximum bets in effect at that particular table. Minimum-bet size may be $2, $3, $5, $10, $15, $25, $50, and $100, but $2 and $3 minimums are often hard to find; the most common table size seems to be $5 or $10. Although maximum bets usually range up to $1,000, pit bosses have special signs available for high rollers, and $2,000 to $5,000 maximums are not unusual. Occasionally, the entire table will be roped off for a really big bettor.

All bets must be placed before any cards are dealt, and many casinos will permit you to place additional wagers in adjacent vacant positions. Procedures for betting more than one hand vary from casino to casino, so check with the dealer if this type of betting appeals to you. Incidentally, when you have finished playing, the dealer can't reconvert your chips into money, but he will be more than willing to change them for larger denominations. The term for that request is "Color me up." For cash, you must take your chips to the cashier's cage.

The Dealer and Game Protocol

Blackjack is played with one to eight decks of cards. Before a new game begins, the dealer spreads the new cards to be used across the table, first facedown so the backs can be inspected for telltale markings, and then faceup, enabling both the dealer and the players to ascertain that there are no extra or missing cards. Refer to Figure 2-1 for the standard blackjack table layout. Standard fifty-two–card, poker-sized decks are used, and the four suits have no significance; only the numerical value of each card is important: twos through nines are counted at their point value, and all tens and face cards are valued at ten. The ace is unique, and can be counted as one or eleven at the player's option.

Then the dealer thoroughly shuffles the decks of cards. Upon finishing, a player is given a colored "cut" card, which is to be inserted anywhere in the stack of cards placed on the table but held by the dealer. Some people prefer not to cut, and the option is then given to the next player. If no one wants to cut, the dealer does it himself. After the cut is completed, the dealer places the colored card toward the back of the stack to indicate when to reshuffle. If it's a single-deck game, the dealer holds the cards and deals; if it's a multideck game, the cards are placed in a wooden or plastic dealing box called a shoe. In any case, the first card—a *burn card*—is not used, but is placed on the bottom of the single deck or in a

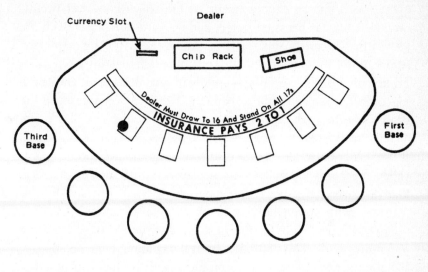

FIGURE 2-1

discard rack. This card is not usually shown, but in many cases the dealer will expose it when a player asks.

Starting with the player on his left, often called *first base*, and continuing in a clockwise direction, the dealer gives each player a card and himself one faceup; then he deals each player a second card, and this time the dealer's card is placed, facedown, under the dealer up card. Both of the players' cards are usually dealt facedown in the single-deck game and faceup in multideck play, but whether the cards are exposed or not, the game is played in the same manner. Although many bettors prefer the single deck, with its feeling of secrecy as they peek at their cards, the trend is overwhelmingly toward the multideck game. Not only is faceup play much faster, and therefore more profitable for the casino, but since bettors are not permitted to touch their cards, the opportunity for player cheating is nearly eliminated.

When everyone has his initial two cards, again starting at first base, each bettor is permitted to draw additional cards, which are always dealt one at a time, faceup. If the player goes over twenty-one, he loses, his bet is collected, and his cards are placed with the rest of the discards. After each player has acted on his hand, the dealer must then complete his own hand based on fixed rules printed on the table covering—usually hitting all sixteens, and standing on all seventeens (the exception is that in some casinos, the dealer hits the "soft" seventeen—ace, six. The dealer's play is not affected by the players' exposed hands; his decisions are mechanical. If the dealer does not go over twenty-one, (going over twenty-one is called *breaking*), he collects from players with hands totaling less than his, pays off players with hands better than his, and ties, or "pushes," with players holding hands of equal value.

Now you are ready for the next hand, which is dealt from the remaining cards. This continues until the colored, cut card appears, signaling a reshuffle after the completion of the hand in progress, and the entire procedure is repeated. As you play, you may notice a well-dressed person with an air of authority casually observing the dealer, the players, and the action; this is the pit boss or floor person who is responsible for a group of tables and settles all disputes. His decisions are final.

Blackjack Terms

Standard blackjack terms are used below to describe how to play the game.

Blackjack. After receiving your initial two cards from the dealer, you determine their value by simply adding them together. A five and three is eight; a king and six is sixteen; and an ace and seven is either eight or eighteen. If your first two cards consist of an ace and a ten or any picture card, the hand is a perfect one—a "blackjack"—often called a "natural." Unless the dealer ties you with another blackjack, you have an automatic winner, and instead of the usual even-money payoff, you are immediately paid one and one-half times your bet. For example, if you have $10 up, you receive $15. With a tie, or "push," no money is exchanged.

Hard and Soft Hands. All hands not containing an ace are known as "hard hands," and any hand including an ace that can be valued as eleven is called a "soft hand." For example, an ace, five is a soft sixteen; if hit with a two, the hand becomes a soft eighteen; if another card is drawn, for instance a nine, the ace is revalued as one (if it was valued as eleven you would break) and the final hand now becomes a hard seventeen. Any hard hand of twelve through sixteen is known as a "stiff," or "breaking hand," because it is possible to go over twenty-one with the addition of one more card.

Objective

Let's now consider the objective of casino blackjack. Many blackjack books define the objective as getting a hand as close as possible to twenty-one. This is not always true. Your objective is to beat the dealer, and learning this lesson is your first step on the road to becoming a winning blackjack player. It is possible to beat the dealer by holding a hand that totals less than twenty-one—even as little as a twelve or thirteen, for example. Remember, there are two ways to win, by holding a higher hand than the dealer, and by not hitting while holding a breaking hand and waiting for the dealer to break. This is a decision that many beginning players seldom make. Thinking they must always get as close as possible to twenty-one, they hit (take extra cards) more often than they should, thus breaking (a hand with a value greater than twenty-one), losing more often, and contributing to the casino edge of up to 6 percent over the nonsystem player.

Casino rules are defined to give the dealer one major advantage and one major disadvantage. His advantage is that he always draws last. If he breaks after you have broken—in reality a tie—he has already collected your chips, and he does not return them. The dealer's disadvantage is that he must draw if he has sixteen or less;

therefore, with hands totaling twelve to sixteen, it's possible that the next card may break him. You, the player, can capitalize on this handicap by making judicious decisions about drawing or standing.

While many players lose because they hit too often, other novices, unrealistically hoping for the dealer to break, do not hit enough. These hitting and standing decisions cannot be made by hunch; logic must be used. If the dealer's up card is two, three, four or five, you know he must hit, no matter what the value of his hole (face-down) card is; therefore, you should stand (refuse any additional cards) on a lower hand value, such as thirteen, and hope for the dealer to break. On the other hand, if the dealer has a high up card, for instance a nine or ten, you would hit and try to get as close to twenty-one as possible because there is a good chance that the dealer's hole card is also high, and with a hand greater than sixteen, the dealer must stand.

Blackjack Decisions

The characteristic that makes blackjack unique among all casino games is the many options a player has to decide on. After you receive your first two cards, in addition to the option of hitting and standing, under certain conditions you are allowed to split your hand, double your bet, insure your hand, or if you are not satisfied with your cards, sometimes you can surrender them and get half your money back. Almost all decisions are indicated to the dealer by the way you move your hand or where you place additional chips after your original wager is made. Let's look at these decisions and their signals; just remember that in Atlantic City and many other places where multidecks are used, you are never permitted to touch your cards or your initial bet.

Standing. The player always has the option of standing at any time. The usual procedure is to give a hand signal rather than a verbal signal. To indicate to the dealer that you wish to stand, simply wave your hand, palm down, over your cards. The dealer will then move on to the next player. In many Nevada games, the cards are dealt facedown and the players pick them up to play the hand. A standing signal in this game is given by tucking your the first two cards dealt (the ones you are holding in your hand) under your chips.

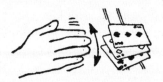

Hitting. If you are not satisfied with the total of your hand, you may draw one or more cards as long as you don't break, or go over twenty-one. To call for a hit, either point at your cards or make a beckoning motion with your fingers. In the Nevada facedown game, scrape your two cards toward you on the felt to call for a hit. When the hit card breaks your hand, the dealer will automatically scoop up your bet and place your cards in the discard tray, as you have lost, even if the dealer subsequently breaks. If you break in the Nevada facedown game, just toss your two held cards to the dealer—faceup.

Splitting Pairs. When the first two cards you receive are of equal value, you may elect to split them and play each as a separate hand, drawing until you are satisfied or you break. You play first the card on your right, and then the card on your left. Two ten-value cards such as a king and jack can also be split, but when aces are split, most casinos permit drawing only one card to each split ace. If a ten-value card is drawn to a split ace, or vice versa, the resulting hand is considered as twenty-one, not a blackjack, and is paid off at one to one. This twenty-one would tie any dealer twenty-one but would lose to a dealer blackjack. In many casinos, if a pair is split and a third card of the same rank is drawn, the hand may be resplit. To indicate to the dealer your desire to split, merely slide up another bet of equal value next to your first wager, touching neither your cards nor the original bet. In the Nevada facedown game, just turn over your pair and put out the extra bet.

Splits   Double Down

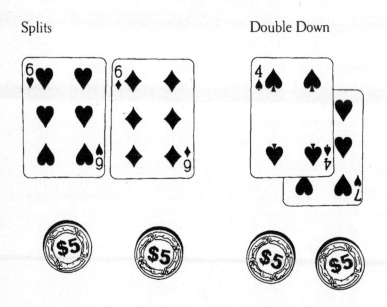

Doubling Down. When you think that with just one more card in addition to your first two you will beat the dealer, you are allowed to double your original bet and draw one, and only one, more card. While many casinos will permit you to double down on any initial hand, except two cards totaling twenty-one of course, some restrict this option to hands that total ten or eleven. To signal the dealer your intention to double, place another bet, up to the amount of the original wager, alongside your first bet. In the Nevada facedown game, turn your two cards over and put out your extra bet. Since you will always have the advantage when you take this option, you should double for the full amount. Again, to minimize the chances of player cheating, you are not permitted to touch either your cards or your original bet. When you split a pair, many casinos will permit you to double down after you draw the first card to each of the split hands.

Insurance. Whenever the dealer's up card is an ace, before proceeding with the hand, he will ask, "Insurance, anyone?" If you believe the dealer's hole card is a ten for a blackjack, you are permitted to place a side bet up to half of your original wager on the insurance line in front of you. If, indeed, the dealer does have a ten in the hole, you are immediately paid two to one on your insurance bet, but lose your original wager unless you too have blackjack and tie the dealer. You are not really insuring anything; you are simply betting that the dealer's unseen card is a ten. The only time I recommend taking insurance is when you have a blackjack and are past the third level of a winning progression (a succession of winning hands). I'll discuss winning progressions in a later chapter.

Surrender. A few casinos offer the option of surrender. If you are not satisfied with your chances of beating the dealer after seeing your first two cards, you may announce, "Surrender"; the dealer will pick up your cards and collect half your bet, returning the other half to you. This is the only decision in blackjack that is indicated verbally. Where the dealer is required to first check his hole card for blackjack, the option is called "late surrender." If you are permitted to turn in your hand before the dealer checks for blackjack, the decision is termed "early surrender." In some casinos, you must announce your surrender decision before the dealer deals to the first hand.

Surrendering before the dealer checks for blackjack is a very advantageous decision for the player because the player only loses half his bet to a dealer blackjack. It is offered in no known casinos as this book goes to press.

Dealer's Play. After offering cards to all players, the dealer exposes his hole card. If there are players who still have not broken, the dealer then acts on his hand according to fixed rules, with none of the player options. When the dealer's cards total seventeen or more, he must stand, and with a hand of sixteen or less, the dealer must hit until he reaches seventeen or better. If the dealer breaks, all remaining players win. In most casinos, the dealer must count an ace in his hand as eleven if it will raise his hand to seventeen, eighteen, nineteen, twenty, or twenty-one. A few casinos make an exception to this rule and require the dealer to hit A, six, or soft seventeen. It is important to note that the dealer has no choice in the matter. If all the players have hands totaling eighteen, nineteen, twenty, or twenty-one, the dealer must still stand with a seventeen — an obvious loser. Likewise, if the players show hands totaling twelve, thirteen, fourteen, or fifteen, the dealer must still hit his sixteen and risk breaking an otherwise winning hand. If the dealer does not break, and reaches a hand between seventeen and twenty-one, proceeding counterclockwise from third base, he collects from players with lower hands, pays off at even money the players with higher hands, and pushes or ties those with equal hands, indicating this with a tap of the back of his fingers in front of the player's cards. Players are now free to pick up winnings, if any, and make a new bet as the whole process is repeated.

The popularity of traditional blackjack is actually diminishing at the beginning of the new millennium. The casinos are introducing variations to traditional blackjack discussed, in Chapter 6, which are competing with blackjack tables for space on the casino floor.

If you are just learning how to play the game, set up a game at home with a spouse or friend. Deal out some hands with this book nearby to insure that you understand all the decisions. Blackjack is a simple game to learn.

Another suggestion for learning the basics of play, is to open an account at an Internet Casino—a no-money account—and play blackjack in the "free play" mode. Don't be tempted, however, to make a deposit yet and play for real money. We'll get to that later after you learn basic strategy and how to win.

Three

THE BASIC STRATEGY FOR PLAYING THE HANDS

DEFINITION

Basic strategy is the term used to denote the correct play for each blackjack hand possibility—the player's hand versus the dealer's upcard. The Basic Strategy was first developed in the 1950s by four mathematicians working on hand calculators: Roger Baldwin, Wilbert Cantey, Herb Maisel, and James P. McDermott. It was published in a book called *Playing Blackjack to Win: A New Strategy for the Game of 21*—a ninety-two–page classic that is now a collector's item. Basic Strategy was refined with computer studies performed over a number of years by other blackjack researchers, the most prominent of whom was Julian Braun. His revisions and improvements were published in his book *How to Play Winning Blackjack*.

Basic Strategy is designed to win more of your good hands and lose fewer of your bad hands; it yields the theoretical best decisions for all the blackjack options—standing, hitting, splitting, doubling, and surrendering. To understand the strategy, though, you must remember the three variables involved in making blackjack decisions—your two cards and the dealer's upcard. There are 550 possible combinations of these three variables; therefore, there are

550 different blackjack decisions. Fortunately, many of these decisions are similar and about thirty rules cover all of them.

If you ask fifty blackjack players if they know Basic Strategy, really know it, 90 percent of them would say yes. But pin them down on a decision or two and they usually flunk. How about you? Do you really know Basic Strategy? You should, as it is the starting point for putting your winning foundation into place.

Take this test to see how well you know Basic Strategy. Your hand is shown first and then the dealer's upcard for the typical six-deck game with doubling down after splitting pairs allowed. Write down your decisions below (after all, this is a handbook) or on a separate piece of paper if you wish.

8, 4 versus 3:

6, 3 versus 2:

4, 4 versus 5:

10, 4 versus 7:

A, 6 versus 3:

5, 5 versus 2

Now check your answers against the Basic Strategy chart shown in Figure 3-1 on the following page. Did you get them all right? If you did, you are in the upper 1 percent of all blackjack players. If not, you need to study. Please continue reading and I will show you in this chapter how to learn Basic Strategy so that you can make these decisions automatically.

Basic Strategy for the Multi-Deck Shoe Game
(Doubling Down After Splitting Permitted)

THE DEALER'S UP-CARD

YOUR HAND	2	3	4	5	6	7	8	9	10	A
8	H	H	H	H	H	H	H	H	H	H
9	H	D	D	D	D	H	H	H	H	H
10	D	D	D	D	D	D	D	D	H	H
11	D	D	D	D	D	D	D	D	D	H
12	H	H	S	S	S	H	H	H	H	H
13	S	S	S	S	S	H	H	H	H	H
14	S	S	S	S	S	H	H	H	H	H
15	S	S	S	S	S	H	H	H	H	H
16	S	S	S	S	S	H	H	H	H	H
17	S	S	S	S	S	S	S	S	S	S
A,2	H	H	H	D	D	H	H	H	H	H
A,3	H	H	H	D	D	H	H	H	H	H
A,4	H	H	D	D	D	H	H	H	H	H
A,5	H	H	D	D	D	H	H	H	H	H
A,6	H	D	D	D	D	H	H	H	H	H
A,7	S	D	D	D	D	S	S	H	H	H
A,8	S	S	S	S	S	S	S	S	S	S
A,9	S	S	S	S	S	S	S	S	S	S
A,A	P	P	P	P	P	P	P	P	P	P
2,2	P	P	P	P	P	P	H	H	H	H
3,3	P	P	P	P	P	P	H	H	H	H
4,4	H	H	H	P	P	H	H	H	H	H
6,6	P	P	P	P	P	H	H	H	H	H
7,7	P	P	P	P	P	P	H	H	H	H
8,8	P	P	P	P	P	P	P	P	P	P
9,9	P	P	P	P	P	S	P	P	S	S
10,10	S	S	S	S	S	S	S	S	S	S

H = Hit. S = Stand. D = Double Down. P = Split.

FIGURE 3-1

Basic Strategy for the Las Vegas Game
(Single-Deck)

THE DEALER'S UP-CARD

YOUR HAND	2	3	4	5	6	7	8	9	10	A
8	H	H	H	D	D	H	H	H	H	H
9	D	D	D	D	D	H	H	H	H	H
10	D	D	D	D	D	D	D	D	H	H
11	D	D	D	D	D	D	D	D	D	D
12	H	H	S	S	S	H	H	H	H	H
13	S	S	S	S	S	H	H	H	H	H
14	S	S	S	S	S	H	H	H	H	H
15	S	S	S	S	S	H	H	H	H	H
16	S	S	S	S	S	H	H	H	H	H
17	S	S	S	S	S	S	S	S	S	S
A,2	H	H	D	D	D	H	H	H	H	H
A,3	H	H	D	D	D	H	H	H	H	H
A,4	H	H	D	D	D	H	H	H	H	H
A,5	H	H	D	D	D	H	H	H	H	H
A,6	D	D	D	D	D	H	H	H	H	H
A,7	S	D	D	D	D	S	S	H	H	S
A,8	S	S	S	S	D	S	S	S	S	S
A,9	S	S	S	S	S	S	S	S	S	S
A,A	P	P	P	P	P	P	P	P	P	P
2,2	H	P	P	P	P	P	H	H	H	H
3,3	H	H	P	P	P	P	H	H	H	H
4,4	H	H	H	D	D	H	H	H	H	H
6,6	P	P	P	P	P	H	H	H	H	H
7,7	P	P	P	P	P	P	H	H	S	H
8,8	P	P	P	P	P	P	P	P	P	P
9,9	P	P	P	P	P	S	P	P	S	S
10,10	S	S	S	S	S	S	S	S	S	S

H = Hit. S = Stand. D = Double Down. P = Split.

FIGURE 3-2

CASINO RULES

The standard casino rules for the multideck shoe games are as follows: double down on the first two cards; double down allowed after splitting pairs; pair splitting allowed up to four hands; aces may be split only once and only one card allowed on each ace, dealer stands on soft seventeen (A, six), insurance allowed, but not surrender. In a few casinos, doubling down after pair splitting is not allowed, and this variation is described below.

The standard casino rules for the single-deck game are as follows: double down on the first two cards; pair splitting up to four hands; aces may be split only once and only one card allowed on each ace; dealer hits soft seventeen (A, six); and insurance allowed, but not surrender.

The small differences between the strategies result from the use of more decks in the game. In general, the multideck strategy is more conservative than the single-deck strategy. An example is the player hand of eleven vs. a dealer up-card of ace. In the single-deck game, with just fifty-two cards, the player has a better chance of drawing the ten, so the correct Basic Strategy play is to double down. More cards in the shoe game reduce the player's chances of drawing a ten, so the correct play is to hit. Refer to the chart in Figure 3-2 for the single deck Basic Strategy.

In some shoe games, players are not allowed to double down after splitting pairs. What this rule variation means is that in these games the player will split fewer pairs because of the advantage of doubling after splitting. A pair of fours, for example, would be split on certain up-cards if doubling after splitting is allowed, but not split if the double down rule is not allowed.

Variations to Basic Strategy for Different Casino Rules:

Here are the pair-splitting rules for shoe games, which do not allow doubling down after splitting pairs:

2, 2: Split on dealer up cards 3–7, not 2–7

3, 3: Split on dealer up cards 4–7, not 2–7

4, 4: Hit on dealer up cards 5–6, do not split

6, 6: Split on dealer up cards 3–6, not 2–6

If the casino permits surrender in the shoe game, surrender the following hands:

9, 7 and 10, 6 against a dealer up-card of ace

9, 6; 9, 7; 10, 5; 10, 6 against a dealer up card of 10 or face card

9, 7 and 10, 6 against a dealer up-card of 9

If the casino allows surrender in the single-deck game, use the shoe strategy above, but also surrender seven, seven against a dealer up-card of ten.

The standard multideck strategy can be used in the two-deck game with the following exceptions:

For hands totaling nine, double down on dealer upcards from two to six, not three to six, five, six or seven, four: Double down against a dealer ace (hit if your eleven is nine, two, or eight, three).

Other Deviations to Basic Strategy

Many blackjack books advise you to never deviate from Basic Strategy. Their reasoning is that you should always make the correct mathematical play for each and every hand. This reasoning is correct if you play for the long term. In this book, however, I am teaching you to play for the *short term*. There are occasions when you should deviate from Basic Strategy, either to protect your locked up, short-term profits, or to avoid risking them on hands with high bets. For example, the Takedown strategy in Chapter 13 advises you to avoid doubling down under certain conditions associated with higher betting levels. A risk-averse Basic Strategy is also described in Chapter 13, the foundation of which is laid in Chapter 10.

I recommend that you learn Basic Strategy thoroughly so that you can play the hands automatically, without even thinking about them. Basic Strategy deviations occur infrequently, and *if you are uncertain about how to play any hand, Basic Strategy is always the correct play*. If you would like a wallet-size card to carry with you on your casino visits, I will be happy to send you one for no charge. Just use the form in the back of this book to request it.

HOW TO LEARN BASIC STRATEGY

The drills and study procedures in this section are taken from my Basic Strategy Home-Study Course.

General Memory Aids

Here are some tricks to help you memorize Basic Strategy for the shoe game. For hitting and standing decisions, think in terms of low cards (two–six) and high cards (seven–A) for the dealer's upcard. When the dealer shows a low card, you would never hit a breaking hand (twelve–sixteen) with the exception of hitting twelve with a two or three showing. When the dealer shows a high card, always assume that his hole card is ten. Then it will be easy to remember that you must keep hitting your hand until you get hard seventeen or better to beat the dealer's potential standing hand. For doubling down on a hand totaling nine, remember that you double on dealer upcards three–six; their sum is nine. For doubling on the soft hands, there is a pattern that will help you remember. For the lower soft hands (A, two and A, three), you double down on five and six only. For the middle pair (A, four and A, five), you add an upcard and double down on four, five, and six. And for the upper pair (A, six and A, seven), add an upcard on the lower end: double down on three, four, five, and six.

Doubling down rules for hands totaling ten and eleven can be remembered as doubling on all up-cards below the number: ten is doubled on two–nine, eleven is doubled on two–ten. Pair-split decisions can be remembered in groups. Twos, threes and sevens are always split on dealer upcards two–seven when doubling down after splitting is allowed. You can remember: twos, threes, sevens: two–seven. Nines (split on dealer upcards of two–nine except seven) are easy to remember if you understand why the seven is left out. A pair of nines is eighteen and will beat the dealer's potential seventeen. Sixes (split on dealer up-cards of two–six when doubling after splitting is allowed) can be remembered as sixes to the six (two–six). For a pair of fours, the memory aid is "four, five, six." Fours are split on five and six when doubling after splitting is allowed.

Finally, on pair splits, remember aces and eights are always split; fives and tens are never split.

Basic Strategy Rules for Hands Containing Three or More Cards

The following two rules apply for hard hands:

- Rule 1: Any multicard hand that totals eleven or less is hit.

- Rule 2: Any multicard hand that totals twelve–twenty-one is played using the hitting/standing strategy.

For multicard soft hands, the following three rules apply:

- Rule 3: Always hit soft seventeen or less. An example of a multicard soft seventeen is: A, two, four.

- Rule 4: Always stand on soft nineteen or higher. An example of a multicard soft nineteen is A, five, three.

- Rule 5: For soft eighteen stand on dealer up-cards two–eight; hit on dealer up-cards of nine, ten, and ace. An example of a multicard soft eighteen is A, three, four.

  Note: should your soft hand turn hard, use Rules 1 and 2. For example: A, two, two hit with an eight becomes a hard thirteen and you would use Rule 2.

Basic Strategy Learning Drills

1. Basic Strategy Deck Drill

Using a single-deck of cards, place one card faceup in front of you; this is the dealer's upcard. Now flip over two cards at a time. Each of these two-card pairs is your hand. Make a Basic Strategy decision for each hand against this same upcard. Deal through the entire deck. Now shuffle the deck, change the upcard and repeat the drill. Choose upcards that may be giving you memory problems.

Do not play out the dealer's hand in this drill.

An alternative procedure for this drill is to deal three cards at a time: an up-card and your two-card hand. Play against a different up-card for each two-card hand dealt.

This drill can be varied to work on various aspects of basic strategy. For example, to practice pair splits, set up a special training deck loaded with extra twos, threes, fours, fives, sixes, and sevens. To practice doubling on nine, ten, and eleven, load up a training deck with extra fours, fives, and sixes.

To practice playing stiff hands, load up a training deck with extra ten-value cards and remove all neutral cards (sevens, eights, and nines). This drill is limited only by your imagination.

2. Basic Strategy Soft-Hand Drill

To practice soft hands, give yourself a hand consisting of A, two and play out the hand after giving the dealer an upcard. After playing each hand, push the upcard and the cards dealt to the A, two aside and start over, dealing a new upcard and playing from the A, two as your first two cards.

3. Three-Card-Hand Drill

To practice multicard hands, deal yourself a hand consisting of three, two and play out your hand after dealing the dealer his up-card. You can change the upcard for each hand or keep it constant until the shuffle. To practice playing stiff hands, start with a ten, three instead of a three, two.

4. Basic Strategy Test

On a plain piece of 8½ × 11 paper, write down the basic strategy rules. Start with hitting and standing rules for hard and soft hands; then write down doubling-down rules for hard and soft hands; finally, write down pair-split rules. Check your answers against the Basic Strategy tables in this chapter.

5. Flash Cards

Flash cards are an excellent learning aid. You can make up your own by purchasing some light cardboard stock at your local stationery store. Cut the stock into one- or two-inch squares. Write down each hand on one side and the correct Basic Strategy play for that hand on the reverse. Use the flash cards to test yourself on each hand. For instance, suppose your flash card shows a thirteen as the hand to be played. Recite the correct play for thirteen before turning the flash card over to check yourself: stand on a dealer up-card two–six; hit on dealer up-card of seven or higher. Use the enclosed Information Request Form if you would like to order a set of flash cards through my office.

Two of the most important aspects of your winning foundation concern money management and discipline. The next two chapters may be the most important in this book. I urge you to study them carefully and incorporate the data into each of your blackjack playing sessions.

Four

How to Create and Manage a Blackjack Bankroll

Before I teach you specific winning strategies, it is necessary for you to learn the fundamentals of money management in this chapter and the essentials of mental preparation in the next.

The advice in this chapter is suitable for both the new-era player and the long-term player.

CREATING YOUR BANKROLL

Most gamblers have no concept of what a bankroll is. When they go to the casino, they grab whatever spare money they can get their hands on and hope for the best. If they go with $100 or $200 and lose the entire amount (which happens most of the time), they "create" another bankroll the next time they decide to visit the casino by grabbing more money they cannot afford to lose. They keep no records and have no idea how much they have lost over their last few trips, during the last month, or the last year. For a number of reasons, this is the wrong way to go. An important step on your road to becoming a winner is to treat your bankroll with respect. But first things first. The first step is to define a bankroll, the second is to show you how to create one.

THE BANKROLL

Let's first discuss what a bankroll is not. It is not money you can get with a credit card. It is not money you have coming to you such as an income-tax refund. It is not what you intend to save over the next few weeks. It is not money you have in the bank or in a savings account. And, except under certain circumstances, which will be discussed below, it is not casino credit.

A bankroll is cold, hard cash you have put together for the purpose of gambling. It is kept separate from your other monies; separate from monies you use for living expenses or monies you have set aside for investment purposes. You should keep your bankroll in a safe place. I suggest, depending on size, you keep it in a safe at home or a safe deposit box at the bank.

Now, if you don't like handling and carrying cash, I suggest the following: Open a line of credit with the casino for a minimum amount. This amount should depend on your financial circumstances, for example $500. When you go to the casino, write a marker for $500. This is your bankroll. When you leave to go home and have won money, be sure to buy the marker back. If you have lost and have less than the $500 left at the end of your trip, the $500 marker will either be treated as a check and sent to your bank for collection or you will be sent a bill for the amount. Treat your credit line with respect and don't be tempted to increase the line to an amount with which you are not comfortable. I would suggest that the amount be no more than 2 percent of your annual salary. If you are making $25,000, that would equal a line of credit of $500; $50,000 would equal a credit line of $1000; and so on.

The epitome of bankroll creation occurred in the late 1980s by one of my students, who called himself "The Equalizer." He created a bankroll out of thin air, with zero of his own dollars! He did this by collecting the casino promotional coupons, free nickels, match play coupons, etc. After collecting his first $10, he began play by betting $1 units and following all of my recommendations for money management and discipline. He lived in Reno, so his over-head was nil, but by using money management and discipline, he created a bankroll of one hundred units after just a few months of play. Small units, yes, but it shows you what can be done with money management, discipline, and a plan. I am not recommend-ing that you create a bankroll out of thin air like The Equalizer; what I am recommending is that you have a plan for creating one.

Terms You Should Know

Now that we have defined a bankroll, let's define the related terms: *betting unit, session bankroll, stop-loss,* and *stop-win.* Make a note of these terms, especially betting unit, because we will be re-ferring to them in subsequent chapters.

Betting Unit. This is your minimum bet, the bet you start with when you enter a game. It can be $1, $2, $5, $10, $25, or higher. Divide your bankroll by one hundred or two hundred to get your betting unit. For a bankroll of $500, your betting unit is $500/100 = $5. For a bankroll of $1000 your betting unit is $1000/ 100 or $10. If you are conservative and want to bet less aggressively, use two hundred as your divisor. For example, $1000 divided by two hundred is a $5 betting unit.

Session Bankroll. This is defined as 20 percent, or one-fifth, of your bankroll. If you are playing with a bankroll of $1000, your session bankroll is $1000 divided by five, or $200. This amount is also your session *stop-loss.* If you lose the $200, you terminate the session. I recommend limiting your gambling-session duration to no more than two hours; anything more and you may start to lose control. At the end of a session, or if you drop a session bankroll, take a break for at least an hour. Go out and take a walk on the Boardwalk or the Strip, have a cup of coffee or take in a bar show. This advice is crucial because it keeps you in control. If you lose your session bankroll and immediately go into your pocket for extra money, who's in control? You or the casino?

What is your table stop-loss? It is three–six betting units and, in no case, more than one-third of your session bankroll. Get up and leave the table immediately when this stop-loss is touched. Find another table. Some tables are simply "cold."

What is your *stop-win*? Let's also discuss this in terms of a *session stop-win* and a *trip stop-win*. Your session stop-win is equal to your session bankroll. If your session bankroll is $200, this amount is your winning goal during the session. More conservative gamblers can shoot for 50 percent of session bankroll; it's up to you. The important idea is to set a goal and stick to it. When you win this amount, terminate your session; take a break and enjoy your win. There is one exception to this rule: If you are in a hot table and winning, stay until it cools off. How do you know when it cools off? When you have given back **no more than** one-third of your winnings. If you are up $300, for example, leave with at least $200 profits in hand.

I realize that many gamblers can't raise more than $100 or $200 for their initial bankrolls. However, I do advise waiting until your bankroll is at a sufficient level to justify a betting unit with the above rules. Nevertheless, some gamblers will take their shot anyway. Here is the money-management strategy for small-bankroll players:

Divide your bankroll into fifty betting units. A $100 bankroll is fifty $2 units; a $250 bankroll is fifty $5 units.

Divide your fifty units into ten table bankrolls of five units each. Do not deviate from this five-unit stop-loss per table under any circumstances, even if it means not doubling or splitting pairs. Follow the Takedown Strategy in Chapter 13.

ENERGY LEVEL—HOW IT AFFECTS YOUR PLAY

You must never, never play when you are tired. This is when you are most likely to lose your self-control. Play when your level of energy is high and when you feel well. Try to stick to the same eating habits as you do at home, consuming similar food at similar times. Be aware of your blood-sugar level. If you have low-blood-sugar syndrome—hypoglycemia—you may get tired at certain times of the day because of a lack of food intake. You can monitor your energy level at home before your casino visit to determine if you get these tired periods. Your doctor can advise you on blood-sugar tests to help define and solve the problem with proper diet and eating habits.

Be very, very careful with your alcohol consumption. Too much alcohol is the easiest way to lose your self-control. If you've had a few cocktails with dinner and feel like you can win the house, do me and yourself a favor and take just one session bankroll with you and give the rest to your spouse or a friend or leave it in a safe deposit box. All casinos have them.

DISASTER: WHAT TO DO IF YOU LOSE YOUR SELF-CONTROL AND DROP THE ENTIRE BANKROLL

If you follow the winning programs in this book, and especially the advice in this and the next chapter, you will not need the advice in this section. Having said that, just about every gambler I know, every student coming into my school, has had this happen at one time or another. So read this section carefully; file it away for future reference, but resolve that you will not need to use it.

You've come to town for the weekend on Friday evening with a $1000 bankroll. By Saturday evening you've had five disastrous sessions and dropped it all. What do you do? If you drove in, run for your car and head for home. If you are waiting for a bus or a plane, find a way to pass the time without rolling a credit card or signing a marker. Treat yourself to a gourmet dinner and take in a show. Believe me, this will prove cheaper than risking any more of your hard-earned money at the tables. Do *not* go to a restaurant inside the casino. Look in the Yellow Pages and pick a restaurant in town. Don't leave yourself open to temptation.

On Sunday morning, take a bicycle ride on the Boardwalk if you're in Atlantic City (from 8 A.M. to 10 A.M. bikes are allowed). If you are in Las Vegas, drive up to Hoover Dam or, better yet, take a ride to Valley of the Fire (about a forty-five-minute drive, beautiful country and well worth your time). There are plenty of places to stop and look and to hike if you are so inclined. I guarantee you will love Valley of the Fire. Most visitors to Las Vegas never give it a thought because it interferes with their action. But you have to take time to smell the roses. And practice your self-control.

If you are in Reno, drive to "the Lake" (Lake Tahoe). Or drive to Virginia City. The old mining town reeks of history and interesting sights.

If you can survive this kind of gambling disaster and make a positive experience out of it, you will look forward to your next trip with the knowledge that you possess the self-control to become a winner.

And be sure to read and follow the advice in the next chapter!

SHOULD YOU TIP THE DEALER?

The subject of tipping is an important part of money management. This is because every time you tip, you either reduce your win or increase your loss. Let me teach you how to let the casinos pay for your tips and maximize the tips you give the dealer.

Make a bet for the dealer but don't put the bet in front of the betting circle on the blackjack table. If you do this, the dealer controls the money, not you. Put the dealer's bet on top of your own.

Announce this to the dealer: "You're riding along with me on this hand." If you lose the bet, that's the end of it. The dealer has lost, too. But he or she knows that you made the bet because you announced it.

Now if you win, you have one of two choices. Let's say you bet $1 for the dealer. Put it on top of your bet as defined in the prior paragraph. Assume you win the bet. You can immediately give the $1 won to the dealer after the payoff and leave the original $1 you bet up for the next hand.

Or you can bet the dollar you just won for the dealer on the next hand and let the dealer control that bet while you leave the original $1 bet on top of your bet for the next hand. I prefer the latter because it gives the dealer a chance to win $2 instead of $1.

The casino forces the dealers to take their bets down after each hand. Why? Because on a hot hand they don't want the dealers profiting along with the gamblers. But when you control the tip money, the dealer rides right along with you. And they really appreciate it. If you don't understand the above discussion, take out some plastic chips and walk through it a few times. It's easy. And it will save you a lot of money. This is because a $1 bet can become $10 or more for the dealer on a series of winning hands. Now you are tipping with money won from the casino, not your wallet.

CASINO COMPS, RATINGS, AND COMP CARDS

A discussion of casino comps in a chapter on money management? Certainly! "Comps" is the jargon for complimentaries or "freebies" given by the casinos to keep the patrons there as long as possible, tempt them into betting more money, and encourage them to come back when they leave. I have seen a cup of coffee cost a gambler hundreds of dollars. Why? Because he waited for it. When the pit boss comps you to dinner, it takes him some time to get the approval. In the meantime, you may be playing at a losing table.

But you wait for the comp. And lose a couple of hundred more. Is it worth it? Of course not! If you are ready to leave the table on a losing streak, leave! Don't wait for the coffee or the comp. If the comp is in the works, check back with the pit boss later. Leave the table and let him know: "I'll check back with you."

In most casinos, if you are betting any kind of money (or "action") at all, the pit announces to you that they are "rating" you. All this means is that they watch your action and record your average bet size, total action, and win and loss in the computer. They use this data to determine whether or not they will comp you and for how much. But this policy encourages gamblers to play for the house and ignore their own money-management policies. I have seen numerous gamblers play beyond a stop-loss just because they were being rated. This is silly! No, it's more than that; it's stupid! It's okay to be rated, but walk away when you are ready to walk. Don't worry about your rating.

The same advice applies to the comp cards pit personnel hand out in many casinos. The purpose of the comp cards is to encourage you to get rated, build up a record of time and action, and qualify for comps. This is fine and you should take advantage of the casinos' generosity. But on your terms, not theirs. Leave the table on a table stop-loss and forget about the rating. It can be detrimental to your bankroll.

MONEY CONTROL

When you are in a game, you should be aware of how much money you have in front of you. Suppose you buy into a game for $100 and run into a hot table. The dealer is breaking and your winning chips are accumulating on the table. You have $1 chips and $5 chips mixed together, and you have no idea how much you actually won. Now the dealer starts winning and you begin to give some of the chips back. If you are not careful, you might lose all the money you just won simply because you don't know how to "control" your money.

Here is the solution. When you are winning, the first thing to do is separate your buy-in from your winnings and place it into a separate stack. Count your winnings when the shoe is being shuffled. Use different-colored chips for stop-win amounts. (For example, use a white $1 chip to segregate $100 of winnings from the rest of your winnings.) You can also put your stop-win (the amount you have "locked up" and will not dip into at this table) in a different spot on the table to separate it from other winnings you are playing with. When you hit a stop-win, leave the table. Money control is extremely important in making these critical decisions and is a key to gaining the winning edge. Practice it!

SUMMARY OF WINNING TIPS AND IDEAS

Because of the importance of money management, let's summarize what you have learned in this chapter.

- Create your bankroll from cash you can afford to lose and store it in a safe place.

- If you prefer not to carry cash, open up a minimum line of credit that does not exceed 2 percent of your annual income. Respect your credit line and do not abuse it.

- Define the betting unit for the level of risk you wish to take: to determine your betting unit, divide your bankroll by two hundred if you are conservative or one hundred if you wish to take more risk. Gamblers with small bankrolls of $250 or less should divide them into fifty betting units.

- Remember these two bankroll divisor numbers as you move ahead to subsequent chapters in this book: two hundred and one hundred. These numbers are for new-era players, not traditional card counters. You will learn in a later chapter that traditional players playing to the long run divide their bankrolls by one thousand, in some cases two thousand, to establish their betting units. Consider the difference in establishing a $10 betting unit; new-era players need $1,000 to support this unit while long-term traditional card counters need $10,000. Quite a difference isn't it? You will learn the why of this in a later chapter.

- Define your session bankroll and your stop-loss for any session as 20 percent of your casino bankroll. Keep your session duration to two hours or less. If you double your session bankroll, terminate your session, take a break, and enjoy your win.

- When you are in a winning streak at one table, give back no more than one-third of the money you have won at this table before leaving the table.

- A table departure is triggered by losing one-third of your session bankroll or a stop-loss of three–six units.

- Never play when you are tired.

- Don't be tempted to use credit cards or cash checks if you drop your entire bankroll. Relax and enjoy the local sights.

- Tip the dealer by controlling his or her bet with your bet, rather than by making a separate bet for him or her.

- Don't wait at a losing table for a comp. Come back for it.

- Practice sound money-control principles as defined in this chapter.

Money-Management Worksheet

My initial bankroll is: _____

The bankroll divisor is: _____

My betting unit is: _____

My session bankroll is: _____

My session stop-loss is: _____

My table stop-loss is: _____

My session stop-win is: _____

Comments and ideas for creating my bankroll:

Five

An Easy-to-Use Program for Developing and Executing Mental Discipline

BACKGROUND

In my twenty-four years of teaching gambling systems, I have never failed to offer instruction on money management in the home-study course or classroom. I taught my students how to establish a bankroll and how to bet in relation to their bankroll. Many of them listened to me, practiced their betting procedure, and then went to the casino and did something entirely different. "Why?" I kept asking myself. I knew what they were doing because they called me up to discuss why they had lost. The problems always boiled down to a lack of mental preparation, to the student's inability to operate in a casino environment. Because, let's face it, when you walk into a casino, they want you to play on their terms, not yours. That's why they bombard you with free drinks, loud music, and a colorfully relaxed atmosphere. That's why you play with chips and not money. After all, what's a chip but a piece of plastic? Most gamblers are mesmerized by the typical casino environment and lose all self-control. If they had any kind of game plan at all, they quickly forget it in the excitement of the action. If they lose, they roll a credit card and get more money.

I began to realize that there was a missing link in my instruction—teaching my students how to exercise self-control and mental discipline. I conducted research activities into the psychology of gambling in conjunction with experts in this field whom I had met through my blackjack classes.

The major finding of these research activities is simply this: Mental preparation and self-control are 90 percent of the game! You can learn the fundamentals of the games and how to bet, but if you are not mentally ready to play, your level of risk is just too high.

You've got to realize that many mistakes inside the casinos are the consequence of problems outside the casino. Understanding and dealing with this relationship is very important in establishing your winning foundation and getting on your road to becoming a winner.

Think back. How many times have you felt mesmerized and totally out of control, pulling more money out of your pocket without wanting to, staying at tables longer than you knew you should, playing too many tables and losing more than your session stop-loss? These are the problems that you've got to deal with before you can start winning on a consistent basis.

The bottom line is not just how much you take off the table; it is how much you *don't lose*, how much you *don't give away* to the casino. This aspect of your game plan is just as important as your winning tables. How many times has a big win been nullified by unnecessary losses? This is another example of a problem that must be addressed before we get into the technical skill areas.

Let me give you a framework for preparing mentally for each casino trip and session. Mental preparation consists of following these five steps:

1. Establishing Goals and Objectives

2. Developing and Documenting a Game Plan

3. Practicing Visualization of Goals and Objectives

4. Executing the Plan

5. Monitoring and Evaluating the Plan

STEP 1: ESTABLISH GOALS AND OBJECTIVES

First answer the question: Why am I gambling? For fun? To get away once in a while from a stressful environment? To feel the rush of an adrenaline high? To make money and win on a consistent basis? To make a living? Most people gamble for fun and enjoyment, but others are more serious about the games. After you answer this question, you can decide what you want to accomplish; what goals you want to realize.

For example, if you wish to gamble to win on a consistent basis or to make a living, you should choose blackjack as your primary game because you can get an advantage over the casino. If you're gambling for fun, you have to decide whether or not you want the action or the money. For example, if your goal is to double your bankroll on a weekend's play, what do you do if this occurs on Saturday and you still have plenty of time left for action? You need to think about and write down these overall goals and objectives. Many high rollers are happy to break even. They get the thrill and glamour of the casino, everything they want for free, and if they play smart, it doesn't cost them a dime.

Let me suggest a goal to you. Build a bankroll. How much money are you playing with now? $500? $1000? Why not establish a goal of building a gambling bankroll of $5000 or $10,000? Then you can live like a king or queen and let the casinos pick up the tab for all your expenses (which they are perfectly willing to do).

When you think about your goals and begin to write them down, be as specific as possible. For example, let's say your goal is to build a $5000 bankroll. Attach a time frame to this goal. Think about what you will do with the money. Your goal might be expressed as follows: "I plan to build a $5000 bankroll within the next six months and use this money as the down payment on a new car." Or—"I plan to build a $5000 bankroll within six months and use it as a permanent blackjack bankroll that allows me to play as a green chip ($25) bettor."

Here are other goals you can consider for your own play:

- Become a professional player
- Let the casinos pay all your expenses and be treated like a VIP
- Become a consistent winner as a part-time player and supplement your income
- Enjoy the action offered by the casinos—break even and avoid heavy losses
- Travel to new blackjack locations and use blackjack winnings to pay for the trip

But establishing a goal is just the first step. Now you must think through how you intend to accomplish the goal. On to Step 2.

STEP 2: DEVELOP AND DOCUMENT A GAME PLAN

After you've listed your goals, decide how you intend to accomplish them. Think about how often you intend to visit the casinos; decide how much money will be in your initial bankroll; buy a spiral-bound notebook and handwrite a page or two. Here is an outline of what to write:

- goals and objectives
- schedule of casino visits
- blackjack methods you intend to master

- mental preparation process you intend to use

- schedule and drills for home practice

- money-management parameters (review money management—Chapter 4)

- typical trip plan including trip duration, casinos to play, and session schedule

You will be surprised at the satisfaction you derive from the simple exercise of writing these items on a page or two of paper. Okay, you have established some goals and you've thought about and planned out how you're going to achieve these goals. What's next? Step 3! It is based on one of Dr. Steve Heller's techniques, called "triggers." Dr. Heller was a well-known southern California applied psychologist who worked with me and my students for many years. He passed away in 1997.

STEP 3: VISUALIZE THE ACHIEVEMENT OF GOALS AND OBJECTIVES

If you have ever read a self-improvement book, you will understand what this is all about. You are asked to visualize in your mind what it is you intend to accomplish. And you are asked to do this on a daily basis or even a few times during the day. Many successful people attribute their success to visualization techniques. Properly used, they can help anyone, especially the casino gambler. Here are a few tips to get you started. Visualize an event that can realistically happen. For example, do not visualize winning $100,000 at the blackjack table, because there is very little chance that will occur.

Take a specific goal such as adhering to a stop-loss. Suppose your session stop-loss is $100 and your objective is to take a one-hour break if you hit that stop-loss. In the past you have not done this, but too often played right through your stop-loss. Visualize yourself walking away from the tables and going out onto the Boardwalk or out into the sunshine and taking a walk. You can also do the opposite and visualize yourself stopping after your win goal has been accomplished. Suppose your goal is to win $500 for the weekend. See yourself winning the $500, terminating your gambling activities, and enjoying the pool and sunshine for the rest of the weekend. Or visualize the win, getting into your car, and driving home. Each visualization should only take a minute or less— actually you can visualize a goal in just a few seconds.

Here is one more tip on doing your visualization exercises. Take one goal, attach a mental picture to it, and visualize it at night before you go to bed. Many studies have proven this to be the most effective hour of the day. However, do not visualize more than one goal at this time. You can visualize one goal for a week or two, until you notice some positive results, and then change to another one.

Triggers

Dr. Steve Heller's Triggers Technique is nothing more than a method for reinforcing positive results; i.e., after doing something right toward accomplishing one of your goals, reinforce it in your subconscious mind so that you can use the good feeling associated with this "win" at a future time when you need it. Here's how: Suppose, for example, that one of your goals is to leave a table after losing six units, something you have had difficulty adhering to in the past. On your next trip to the casino, you decide to make a special effort to follow this stop-loss procedure. Your first table turns out badly, but you feel good about leaving after losing six units. Pick a spot on your body to touch, say the back of your left hand, and touch that spot as you experience the "good feeling." That is your trigger for this goal. Every time you leave a table after losing six units, touch this spot. And feel good about it. Feel good about the discipline of adhering to a stop-loss. You are reinforcing a positive action!

"Now, how do I use this trigger?" you are asking. Here's how.

Suppose you are sitting at a table and are down five units. You double down, lose the hand, and now you're down seven units. You decide to play one more hand because the dealer was just lucky on that last hand and should have never beaten you. But wait a minute! Who's in control here? You or the casino? You touch the back of your left hand and reexperience the positive feelings that are associated with the trigger of leaving the table after a stop-loss. You regain control and leave the table.

At this stage, we have established our blackjack goals, developed a game plan, and visualized the positive outcome of our plan. Now it's time to talk about plan execution, Step 4 of the process.

STEP 4: EXECUTE YOUR GAME PLAN

To execute your game plan, write an agenda much like a travel agent does when he or she schedules a trip, no matter the duration— a day, weekend, or a week. Write everything on paper. Be sure to schedule your gambling sessions on a daily basis. Start each day with the time you arise and end with the time you go to bed. List the casinos at which you intend to play, the time you intend to play, and the duration of each playing session. Show your lunch and dinner breaks. And add the time you intend to take to "smell the roses."

Remember one of the tips from the last chapter—limit your gambling sessions to no more than two hours. If you find yourself getting tired or losing control in any way, don't hesitate to stop before your session time is up. A plan is nothing more than a guideline.

Follow your plan within reason. Obviously, if you are winning heavily at one table, don't leave the table to keep to your schedule.

The purpose of the plan is to put you in control of your gambling activities. When you do this once and execute the plan, you will understand the benefits: It will help you to control your emotions. What you want to accomplish with this step is to play according to your schedule and your requirements—not the casinos'.

STEP 5: MONITOR AND EVALUATE THE EXECUTION OF YOUR GAME PLAN

This is a very important step because it allows you to update your plan with ease. This involves keeping a table-by-table record of your casino play. For example, let's say you play a blackjack table. What was your bankroll going into the table? How long did you play? How much did you win or lose? What was your betting unit? **Carry a pocket notebook and document these items immediately after playing each table!** If your goal is to become a winner, you must do this and you must make it a habit. It only takes a few seconds after each table, but the payoffs are great. Now you can evaluate your play in an unemotional, detached manner after each session. You can determine how well you followed your plan and what problems you encountered. **And you can take corrective action!** The satisfaction you will derive from following this simple procedure will amaze you. Do it!

Here is a summary of the items of information that should be documented for each table you play. You can copy them directly to your pocket notebook as column headings.

- Date

- Time of Day

- Casino Name

- $ Win or Loss
- Cumulative $ Win or Loss for this Session
- Play Duration
- Cumulative Play Duration for this Session
- Comments on this table such as: Mistakes Made, Distractions That Affected Your Play, or Departures from Your Plan

Six

CASINO VARIATIONS TO TRADITIONAL BLACKJACK GAMES

Variations to traditional blackjack games are becoming quite popular for two reasons: (1) the players like them and (2) with a higher house edge, they generate more income for the casino. The three most popular variations are discussed in this chapter. Although I recommend that you focus on traditional blackjack, use this chapter as a reference if you decide to have some fun and take a shot in one of these games.

SPANISH 21

This blackjack variation game is becoming extremely popular and should be around for a while. Spanish 21 offers the player-favorable rule of doubling down on any number of cards, not just your first two. So, if you draw three, four, two, a hand totaling nine, you can double down. Another player-favorable rule is surrender. Surrender your first two cards and lose only half your bet.

Spanish 21 also pays bonuses on the following hands:

- A five-card hand equal to twenty-one pays three to two

- A six-card hand equal to twenty-one pays two to one

- A seven (or more)-card hand equal to twenty-one pays three to one

- A three-card hand of six, seven, eight of mixed suits pays three to two

- A three-card hand of six, seven, eight of the same suit pays two to one

- A three-card hand of six, seven, eight of all spades pays three to one

- A seven, seven, seven hand of mixed suits pays three to two

- A seven, seven, seven hand of the same suit pays two to one

- A seven, seven, seven hand of all spades pays three to one

Very attractive, aren't they? But, as usual, there is a catch (naturally)—a multideck Spanish 21 game contains no tens! Every ten has been removed (just the tens, not the jacks, queens, or kings) from the six- or eight-deck game. If you're playing perfect multideck basic strategy, with no advantage-play strategies, I estimate the casino advantage against you at about 3 percent. Frank Scoblete, in his book *Armada Strategies for Spanish 21,* says he can reduce the house edge to a little less than 1 percent if you learn his hand-playing strategy, which capitalizes on the favorable rules.

Is the game worth it? I don't think so. I believe your time is better spent with the advantage strategies in this book even if you're an occasional gambler. But if you like to make lots of decisions and if you like the bonus-hand payoffs in Spanish 21, you might want to give it a try as a fun diversion from the traditional game.

Decisions Confronting the Spanish 21 Player

Here are examples of some of the decisions confronting the Spanish 21 player and a basic strategy for making them:

Should I double down on a three-card hand or a four-card hand?

The most favorable rule in this game is the one allowing the player to double down on any number of cards instead of just the first two. When your first two cards are soft, such as with an ace, or if your first two cards total less than eight, always anticipate a possible three- or four-card double-down hand.

Should I take a hit with my four-card fifteen against a dealer six up-card in hopes of catching a six for a twenty-one and collecting the three to two bonus?

Let the bonuses come as part of your traditional Basic Strategy play. In other words, do not hit a breaking hand in hopes of getting paid for a five-card twenty-one. Do not hit a breaking hand in hopes of catching a multicard twenty-one, a seven, seven, seven hand, or a six, seven, eight hand.

For example, if your hand is three, two, three, eight against a dealer up-card of six, you might be tempted to go for the five-card twenty-one bonus, but I don't recommend it. Play Basic Strategy and stand. The same advice holds for a hand of six, seven against a five; don't be tempted to go for the six, seven, eight bonus. Follow Basic Strategy and stand.

Another example: If you are dealt two sevens and the dealer's up-card is a six, follow the Basic Strategy of splitting instead of going for the bonus hand.

Should I surrender my two-card sixteen against the dealer's jack up-card?

The Surrender Strategy is based on a game with a normal number of tens, that's sixteen in each fifty-two–card deck. Surrender is not advisable in Spanish 21.

Basic Strategy for Spanish 21

Because the six-deck shoe has twenty-four fewer high cards with the tens removed, your double-down basic strategy rules should be adjusted to eliminate a few double-down hands. This is because of the smaller chance of the player catching a high card to complete the double-down hand, and because of the smaller chance of the dealer catching a high card to break a stiff hand. Therefore, if your two-card or multicard hand totals nine, double down on dealer up-cards of five and six only, not three–six. For a hand totaling ten, double-down on four–seven only, not two–nine. And, for a hand totaling eleven, double-down on three–eight only, not two–ten.

For soft hands—hands containing an ace, which can be counted as either one or eleven—you have a choice of going for the bonus on the five-, six-, seven- (or more) card twenty-one or looking for the opportunity of doubling down. Which do you choose? Opt for the double down. The reason is that to catch the bonus, your hand must total twenty-one exactly. It happens sometimes, but not often enough to pass up a good double-down bet. Use Basic Strategy for doubling down on soft hands. Some soft hands will naturally lead to the opportunity of the multicard twenty-one bonus. For example, if you are faced with a ten up-card with an A, two, and hit this hand with an ace for a soft fourteen, then a two for a soft sixteen, you're in position for a "free shot" at the five-, six-, or seven- (or more) card twenty-one. But now, hitting this six or sixteen with a seven, for example, what do you do? Now you're sitting with a five-card thirteen. Basic Strategy says hit this hand against the ten so you still have one or two more shots to catch the multicard twenty-one as part of your Basic Strategy play.

Basic Strategy rules for hitting the stiff hands thirteen–sixteen should be adjusted to factor in the fewer tens in the game. Play these stiff hands the same way you would play a twelve — hit on a dealer up-card of two and three; stand on a dealer up-card of four, five, and six.

Add one hand to the Basic Strategy surrender rules described in this chapter — surrender a pair of eights against a dealer up-card of ace.

If you're in the game and in doubt about the Basic Strategy adjustments recommended here, play basic strategy.

MULTIPLE ACTION BLACKJACK

This is one of my favorite variations of blackjack. In this game, you are playing your dealt hand, with two or three bets, against three different dealer hands, but all starting with the same up-card. The game begins with the players placing either two or three bets in three betting circles in front of each player's seat. Let's say the dealer deals himself a five while you're sitting with a fifteen. Basic Strategy says you should stand.

After all of the players make their decisions, the dealer completes this hand. Let's say he breaks. This is Hand 1, and the dealer pays off the players left in the game (those who have not broken and lost).

Now comes Hand 2. You play your same hand, but the dealer must deal himself a new hand starting with that same five up-card. This hand is completed and then a third hand is dealt in the same way, with you keeping your same hand and the dealer dealing another hand to that five up-card.

Going back to your hand of fifteen, if you hit that fifteen, let's say against a ten up-card, you lose all three bets and now must wait for the round of three hands to be completed and another to begin.

This game is really fun when you find yourself in a dealer-breaking table (see Chapter 13 for a discussion). The characteristics of a dealer-breaking table are low up-cards that turn into stiff hands (twelve–sixteen) and then the dealer breaks. Instead of winning just one hand, now you're winning three. The winning can pile up fast in a multiple-action game. If you play this game, use Basic Strategy to play your hands, and use the betting tactics described in Chapter 3.

DOUBLE EXPOSURE BLACKJACK

Another game that was extremely popular in the 1980s and is still around in a few casinos is called Double Exposure. In this variation, the dealer shows both his cards, instead of one card up and one card down. In a traditional game, this rule of knowing the dealer's exact hand would give even the Basic Strategy player a huge edge. For example, think about a stiff hand, such as a sixteen, against a ten up-card. Basic strategy says you should hit. But in Double Exposure, seeing that the dealer's hand is also stiff, you stand and leave the dealer with the higher chance of breaking because he must hit sixteen or less.

The catch in this game is when both hands are the same, a push in traditional blackjack, with no money changing hands. In Double Exposure, the dealer wins all pushes, a huge house edge of about 9 percent. Picture yourself with a nineteen against the dealer's nineteen; what do you do? If you stand, you lose the tie bet. You must hit the nineteen with the extremely small chance of catching the ace or deuce. Even though this game is very appealing to the recreational player, there is no way you can realistically beat it. I recommend that you avoid it.

There you have it—three example of variations to traditional casino blackjack games. As time goes on, I suspect the casinos will continue to introduce new variations to traditional blackjack. If you play them, take care! One thing you can always be sure of is that they will be very advantageous to the house.

Section Two

EVOLUTION OF BLACKJACK SYSTEMS AND METHODS

Seven

CARD-COUNTING PROS AND CONS

A BRIEF LESSON ON CARD COUNTING

Since there is a long history behind the tradition of card counting and its recognition as a valid strategy, I feel I should give you some basic information about how to count. Once you understand the concept, you can understand the problems with card counting, which will be discussed next. The use of card counting in systems unique to this book is discussed in Section 3.

Standard High-Low Point-Count System

Counting does not take a good memory because there is nothing to memorize. All you have to understand is that there are high cards, low cards, and neutral cards in a fifty-two–card deck. In fact, there is an equal number of high and low cards. In the standard High-Low Point-Count System, low cards are two through six; high cards are tens, picture, and aces; neutral cards are sevens, eights, and nines.

Here are the values of these three categories of cards: two through six = +1; tens, pictures and aces = −1; sevens, eights, and nines = 0.

Starting with zero off the top of a deck of cards or dealing shoe, all you do is add 1 for each low card you see dealt, subtract a 1 for every high card you see dealt, and repeat the count so you won't forget it when you see a neutral card, or 0. As the count goes up, it means there are more low cards being dealt (they have a "plus" value) and more high cards left in the shoe remaining to be dealt. If the count is minus, it means that there are more low cards in the shoe remaining to be dealt.

Since a shoe rich in high cards favors the player (for example, a better chance of drawing a blackjack) and a shoe rich in low cards favors the dealer (who will therefore break less often and win more hands), the count gives the player a mathematical assessment of his or her chances of winning the next hand. If his chances are good, the bet is increased. If they are poor, the player makes a minimum bet.

The Plus Count

The plus count is a consequence of more low cards being dealt than high cards, and since there is an equal number of each in the deck, a plus count means that there are more tens and aces remaining in the deck to be played than low cards. This creates the possibilities of more player blackjacks with the payoff of 1.5 to 1 (the dealer gets no such payoff on his blackjacks), more dealer breaking on stiff hands (hands totaling twelve through sixteen; rules of play stipulate that the dealer must hit his hand until it totals seventeen or more), and more double-down wins (the doubling of a bet on the first two cards) for the player (for example, drawing a ten-value card to an eleven for a hand totaling twenty-one).

Essentially, the player is betting more when he has the advantage, and less when the dealer has the advantage. Therefore, a profit is realized over the long run. The count can also be used to play the hand, but this tactic is beyond the scope of this brief lesson and will be taken up in Chapter 15.

Other Card-Counting Systems

With the increasing popularity of the game following the opening of the Atlantic City casinos, research projects multiplied. Some of this research was done by college professors who rarely, if ever, saw the inside of a casino. And some was performed by blackjack players with statistical skills who enjoyed figuring out Basic Strategy play to the third decimal place (a neat academic exercise but hardly useful inside a casino).

The initial thrust focused on the development of point-count systems that determined the optimum values to assign the various cards to maximize the players' theoretical advantage. Arguments went on among these researchers for years as to the merits of the various levels of point-count systems and about the values of the points assigned to each card. For example, a Level I system would assign the numbers 1, −1, and 0 to the card types while a Level II system would assign 1, −1, 2, −2, and 0. Level IV was the highest of the levels with values from +4 to −4.

Recommendation

My recommendation to you in the original edition of this book still stands: If you decide to learn how to count, learn the High-Low Point-Count System described earlier in this chapter. If you have learned a Level I count with the ace valued as −1, do not change; your count will work just as well as High-Low. If you have learned a single-level count with the ace valued as zero, change your point-count assignments to agree with High-Low: two–six = +1; 7, 8, 9 = 0; tens, face cards, and aces = −1.

If you have learned a multiple-level count, I recommend that you discard it and learn High-Low. Here are two reasons why:

1. Many advanced, multiple-level count systems count the ace as zero. The ace is the most important card in the deck. If it's assigned a value of zero, it has a neutral value. Therefore, to achieve maxi-

mum effectiveness from your point-count system, you must keep a side count of aces and factor this side count into your betting and playing decisions. Even professional blackjack players have difficulty with this practice. Recreational players who try it are prone to error.

That leaves us with two choices for the ace: assign it a value of +1 and call it a small card. Or assign it a value of −1 and call it a high card. There was a system published in the early days of card counting called the "One/two Count" that valued tens at −2 and all others, including the ace, as +1. It was an attempt to transform Thorp's Ten Count System (as published in his book *Beat the Dealer*—reviewed in Chapter 11) to a Point-Count System. It did not work except in a single-deck game. Research and computer studies showed that the level of betting and playing effectiveness was sharply reduced when this system was employed. The best approach is to define the ace as a high card and assign it a value of −1.

2. If you are considering learning an advanced point-count system such as the Revere APC or the Uston APC, here are my comments based on conversations with hundreds of blackjack players and my own thirty-five years of casino blackjack experience. Don't do it. First of all, it will take you hundreds of hours to practice and perfect all the nuances for using the count to bet and play the hands. Secondly, the small additional paper advantage you gain will quickly evaporate in the real world of casino play. I have talked to players who have spent months practicing an advanced point-count system only to go to the casino and crumble under the pressure of making split-second decisions. When they call me for advice, it is difficult to tell them they have wasted their time, but this is what I have to do. Many of those who followed my advice have gone on to become consistent winning players.

WHY THE COUNT DOES NOT ALWAYS WORK

The evolution of blackjack systems and methods in the 1980s unfolded along two major research pathways: Pathway 1 — changes to card-counting systems and methods; and Pathway 2 — changes engendered by the recognition of the nonrandom shuffle and its impact on the *application of systems and methods in the real world of casino play.* I was involved in both of these pathways and the major cause of the diversion of Pathway 2. I will now discuss how this diversion came about and how it rendered many strategies in Pathway 1 ineffective. It is important for you to understand this diversion to Pathway 2 now so you can better understand the new strategies presented later. First, however, some background:

My recognition that card counting doesn't always work did not happen overnight. It started with two incidents. The first was a chance conversation I had with a blackjack player in a business supply store a number of years ago. I had stopped in to pick up some office supplies, and the proprietor, knowing me as a blackjack instructor and knowing the other fellow as a player, naturally introduced us. We got to talking and this guy told me that I had the game figured out all wrong.

"Why bet up when the count is rising?" he said. "This is when the low cards are coming out and the dealer has the advantage."

"But there are more high cards left in the shoe and you have a better chance of getting one," I countered. "Everybody knows that more high cards left in the shoe gives the player a greater chance of winning — he will be dealt more blackjacks, win more double downs, and the dealer will break more often on stiff hands."

"You've got it backward," he said. "I bet up when the count is minus and when more high cards are coming out."

I dismissed this guy as a nut, left the store, and forgot all about it until about ten days later when I was in what was then the Golden

Nugget (now The Hilton) in Atlantic City and playing in a $25 game. This is when the second incident occurred.

About one deck had been dealt in this six-deck game when the count began to move up very rapidly. (Note to novice players: when the count moves up, it means that more low cards, counted as +1, are being dealt; the player has a mathematical advantage because the remaining shoe is rich in tens, face cards, and aces.) My bet began to move up with the count. I lost a $50 bet. The count continued to move higher. I lost a $100 bet. By this time, three decks have been dealt and the count is +15. The True Count is now +5 (True Count = running count of +15 divided by three decks remaining. The True Count is a mathematical reflection of the odds of winning the next hand). I bet the True Count in my $50 units (a $250 bet). I lost. The count is now +20. I bet $300. I double down with an eleven and draw a three. The dealer shows a seven, turns over an eight, and I feel a surge of adrenaline with this reprieve. Surely with over twenty extra high-cards left in this shoe, the dealer will draw one and break. No such luck. He draws a two for a seventeen. I'm out another $600. The count is now +24 and there are just over two decks left to play before the shuffle. A "True" of around 12 gives me about a 6 percent advantage on the next hand. I bet $500. By this time a crowd has gathered around the table, two of whom are my students who have stopped to watch the master play. What they saw was the master losing another hand.

This shoe got me to thinking about that conversation ten days ago. If my "friend" from the office supply company had been in this game, he would have said, "I told you so." What had happened, as I was later to learn, is that I *played into a clump of low cards*. The extra high cards that my count indicated were in the shoe were never dealt. They were behind the cut card. Without knowing it, I was playing into a devastating dealer advantage!

"So what!" you may be asking, especially if you are an experienced card counter. Anything can happen in a blackjack game. The next time you find yourself in a hot shoe, you could win all that back and then some.

This line of thinking is indeed correct. But, nevertheless, these two incidents led me into a research project the outcome of which totally changed my thinking about the game of blackjack. I learned why the count does not always work.

Consider the case when you are losing on a high count. The reason is this: The count keeps going up because low cards are being dealt. Low cards favor the dealer and you are playing in the midst of a low-card clump. This clump of low cards is a *dealer bias*.

Now consider the case when you are winning on a low count. The count is minus because high cards are being dealt. You are playing in the midst of a high-card clump and winning. This is called a *player bias*.

Things are working out just the opposite of the way they are supposed to, aren't they? Granted, it doesn't always happen this way; in a shoe with well-shuffled cards, the high cards may come out when the count goes up. But in a game with like-card clumping, betting with the count can be devastating because the high cards just don't come out, as low card after low card is dealt and the dealer doesn't break.

These clumps are caused by the *nonrandom shuffle*. Insufficient shuffling of eight, six, or four decks of cards produces favorable or unfavorable clumps that can last from one shoe to the next.

It is very important that you understand fully why card counting doesn't always work. Let's continue this discussion by posing some questions.

QUESTIONS FOR A TRADITIONAL CARD COUNTER

How many times have you sat at a table in a minus-count situation, making minimum bets and winning hand after hand when, according to card-counting theory, you "should have been" losing?

When you left the table with a smaller profit than most of the other "unskilled players," did you question the value of the count since it did not alert you to a winning situation? How much more could you have made if you had raised your bets as the other players at the table did?

How many times have you lost hand after hand in a high count with your maximum bet out? There is no greater frustration than betting up when the count skyrockets only to be beaten by the dealer hand after hand after hand.

Have you ever been the only losing player at a table with a high count? Everyone else kept getting the high cards and you kept getting the poor hands?

Has there ever been a time when you lost a lot of money playing heads-up (just you and the dealer)? When you walked away from the table, did it ever occur to you that the reason no one was playing against that dealer was because the dealer was "hot" and had sent the players scurrying away with their losses?

The reason all these situations develop is because, in the real world of casino blackjack, there is such a thing as a biased game. And there is nothing you can do to change the bias since the cards are already situated. In the real world of casinos and dealers . . .

Card Counting Is No Longer Enough!

I have been showing you in this chapter why card counters have a theoretical mathematical edge over the casinos. And I have posed a very important question: Why does the high count sometimes not work at all, and why does the low count (when you are supposed to lose) sometimes produce winning hands?

Here is a general answer to the question: Some games have a bias in favor of the dealer and some games have a bias in favor of the player.

To give you a specific answer, let me introduce you to the notion of blackjack biases by explaining what I mean by biases and how they affect the count.

BIASES CAUSED BY THE NONRANDOM SHUFFLE

Most blackjack books state that card counting has been tested in the computers and that you will win about 1.5 percent of all the money you bet if you count cards correctly and bet correctly according to the count.

That is very true *if you are playing within the confines of a computer.* In a computer, the cards are never shuffled. There *are* no cards—only random numbers generated by a computer program. The computer program spits out numbers randomly. Random means that, theoretically, each number has the same chance of coming up as any other. This is the kind of game you will find in the Internet Casinos discussed later in this book.

In a major study conducted by Dr. Persi Diaconis, of Harvard University, and Dr. Dave Bayer, a mathematician and computer scientist at Columbia University, it was proven that seven shuffles are necessary to randomly mix a single deck of cards, and that twelve shuffles are necessary to randomly mix six decks of cards (the number of decks found in most shoe games).

In the casino, there is no such thing as randomly shuffled cards. The dealer shuffles between three and five times before dealing a new round in a single-deck game, and once or twice only in a shoe game. The casino's objective is to keep the game going, take your money as quickly as possible, and make room for the next player, who they hope will be another loser. More time spent on the shuffle means more down time, with no bets being made. This costs the casinos money. The type of shuffle employed and the number of times the decks are shuffled is a business decision usually made at the casino manager level. And this decision is usually made to maximize the casino's bottom line.

Comparing the computer-played game of blackjack with random numbers to the real game of blackjack with its nonrandom shuffle is like comparing apples to oranges. Until I realized this, I thought everything was accurate in the card-counting research. In my earlier books, I recommended the High-Low Point Count. I still feel that particular count is the best one for recreational players and professional players because it is simple and easier to use than a multi-level count. That's why we teach it.

But players who understand biases have an advantage over traditional players who use the count only. They can select tables where the count works well because of these biases. When they find a table that has a bias in their favor, the count works better than ever. In Chapter 10, you will learn how to recognize a bias and about a strategy called Target 21 for detecting and exploiting biases.

Card counting and card-counting research projects had a major influence on the evolution of blackjack systems and methods in the 1980s. For example, another major research thrust involved optimal bet sizing with the Kelly Criterion. The Kelly Criterion, simply stated, means that your bet size should be related to your mathematical advantage on the next hand to be played. Computer simulations and complex mathematical formulas were used to determine these bet sizes according to bankroll size and relate them to the True Count, which is a mathematical reflection of the player's odds of winning the next hand.

I participated in a number of these projects and enjoyed them immensely. I used the results of this research to teach an Advanced Card-Counting Clinic and to establish betting guidelines for my blackjack teams.

But I learned something about the Kelly Criterion in the two to three years that I used it: It does not take into account the realities of the cards coming out of a shoe in a real blackjack game. It works well in a computer environment, and it works well in a game with the cards and the count going my way, i.e., "I am winning." But, if I have lost three hands in succession, the dealer is getting the high cards on the high count, and the count keeps going up, Kelly doesn't consider what has happened in these last three hands. Kelly tells me to make an even bigger bet on the next hand, to do what the card counting experts criticize most about noncount systems — increasing the bet on successive losses; i.e., using an up-as-you-lose betting strategy. Kelly is jeopardizing my bankroll!

THE CONTROVERSY BETWEEN THE TRADITIONAL PLAYER AND TODAY'S PLAYER

I have mentioned that there were two major research and development pathways in the 1980s and 1990s: the traditional card-counting pathway (Pathway 1) and the alternative pathway concerned with player biases engendered by the nonrandom shuffle (Pathway 2).

In our discussion of the evolution of blackjack systems and methods in this book, we will review interesting projects on the development of winning blackjack systems from both of these pathways. In your development as a winning blackjack player, it is important that you understand "where we came from" so that you can fully appreciate "where we are going" and make your choice of which pathway you intend to follow.

It is also important for you to be aware that there is a controversy that has evolved over the years between the two camps. It boils down to this:

Traditional Players (Pathway 1) say that there is no basis for basing table entry, betting, and table departure decisions on biases caused by the non-random shuffle. The only way to get an advantage, they say, is to bet the count, without regard to clumps of high or low cards, and to bet and play the hand according to the count. Any swings in the bankroll, according to their posture, will be made up by playing to the long run and letting the mathematics of the game prevail. And, finally, they say, the mathematical advantage of around 1 percent is still possible to achieve in today's casino environment.

Today's Players (Pathway 2) say look at the real-world evidence. Why not recognize the realities of the casino shuffle for the six- and eight-deck shoe games that do produce clumps of cards that can hurt the card counter? Why not minimize the impact of these clumps and, when conditions warrant, why not exploit them in the short run?

The empirical evidence is in, methods are available that mitigate the effect of clumps on the card counters advantage and that can be used on their own without risking the up-as-you-lose betting that card counting dictates for betting in some of these devastating low-card clumps.

Both sides have their proponents and opponents. The card counters are the most vocal, because, in my opinion, they have the most to lose. An industry has been built based on the fact that card counting is the only way to get an edge at blackjack. This industry is driven by the many new books that are written by traditional card counting authors espousing this philosophy—books that if you look outside the 1 percent edge they attempt to perpetuate or to increase by one or two one-hundredth's of a percentage point, are nothing more than rehashes of prior published books. And they represent one of the reasons that almost two hundred blackjack books are now in publication, confusing the newcomer as he or she attempts to decide in which direction to go.

It is interesting that many traditional players have switched sides and wised up; some still use card counting, but recognize when the count should be put aside and caution adopted in some games. But most of the blackjack authors stick with their tunnel vision and pooh-pooh any new ideas that don't conform to their way of thinking as hogwash.

The New-era Players, on the other hand, enjoy the best of both worlds, many using card counting to their advantage in the appropriate situations, others using noncount methods to achieve a real advantage.

This controversy has erupted on the Internet with web sites, list servers, and web rings devoted to both sides of the controversy about which we will have more to say in Chapter 19.

Eight

Team Play: Advanced Blackjack Method From Research Pathway 1

THE ATLANTIC CITY "CANDY STORE"

When Resorts International Casino opened in May of 1978, little did anyone realize at the time the impact this event would have on the development of winning systems to beat the game of casino blackjack. This was because the rules of the game were the most favorable in the world and not only benefited occasional players, but also encouraged skilled and professional players to flock to Atlantic City.

Here is what happened.

In an attempt to give the gaming public a favorable game, the gaming commissioners of the State of New Jersey approved four rules that created what professional blackjack players refer to as a "candy store." These rules existed between May 1978 and September 1981. The first rule was "surrender."

Surrender means giving up your hand after the first two cards are dealt. Your chances of beating the dealer are slim, so you announce the decision orally: "I surrender." The dealer picks up your hand and takes half your bet. The difference between the surrender decision and the early surrender decision involves the dealer's hole card and whether or not the dealer has blackjack. You are not allowed to surrender against a dealer blackjack; in other words, you must lose your entire bet; you cannot surrender and save half of it. But you can early surrender against a blackjack. This is what the *early* means; you surrender early, before the dealer checks the hole card to determine whether or not he has blackjack. According to the mathematics of blackjack, this rule subtracts only about one-tenth of 1 percent from the house advantage over the Basic Strategy player. The second rule change, dealer no-peek, made early surrender possible. This occurred because the second rule prohibited the dealer from checking the hole card (the dealer is dealt one card up and one card down, the down card is called the hole card) until after all the players had played their hands.

To better understand the impact of these two rules, visualize the following hand. You are dealt a ten, six against a dealer's ace upcard. Your chances of winning are very, very small. If you hit the sixteen, you will most likely break. If you stand, the dealer, with an ace, will probably make his or her hand. With an ace showing, the dealer breaks only about 12 percent of the time. But, betting $10 on the hand, you employ the early surrender rule. The dealer scoops up your cards and takes half of your bet, or $5.

When the dealer's turn comes, he turns over a king for a blackjack. Do you see the advantage? You have only lost half your bet against a blackjack!

Blackjack's mathematicians quickly worked out a playing strategy for this very favorable rule, and guess what? Using a mathematically derived strategy for playing the hands, the player now held an advantage over the house! A small but very significant 0.25 percent. The tables had turned.

There's yet a third rule without which the Atlantic City Candy Store would not have opened for business. The dealer was required to deal two-thirds of a shoe before shuffling. Now if you understand card counting, you'll understand how easy it was to win while this Candy Store was open. When the remaining deck to be played, that is, those cards left in the shoe, is rich in tens and aces, the player has an advantage on the next hand. The size of that advantage is determined by the number of extra ten-value cards and aces—the more the better. The player had it all his own way; the third rule prohibited the dealer from shuffling up when the card counter raised his bet on hands on which he held the advantage. For example, if the count determined that the dealer had the advantage on the next hand, the counter might bet $5. But if the counter held the advantage on the next hand, he might bet $100 or more.

Put these three rules together with a fourth rule that said the casinos were not allowed to bar blackjack players from play, and you have the most favorable blackjack game ever offered in this country. For instance, if you raise your bet from $5 to $100 in Nevada, the pit boss comes over and announces, "that's your last hand," and politely shows you to the door. But not so in Atlantic City in these early days of "the candy store." You could raise your bet to table maximum if your bankroll permitted it, and they couldn't do anything but grit their teeth and watch you rake the chips off the table. (This no-barring rule was reversed in early 1979.)

This game was made to order for blackjack teams, and they began invading Atlantic City in earnest in December of 1979.

At the time, Team Play was the most powerful and most feared of all of blackjack's winning weapons. It is still a usable technique today, and I will show you how after explaining what it is and how it works.

How Team Play Works

Consider the following scenario:

You are a card counter sitting at a blackjack table, patiently counting down the deck and waiting for a favorable situation to develop. But let's assume the high cards and aces are played early in the shoe and you never get that favorable situation during the entire shoe. You've spent a lot of wasted time.

But now let's change the scenario. You are a big player with a team of counters deployed throughout the casino. One of your counters gives you a signal to enter the game and then signals a very high count. The pit bosses don't know what's going on because no words are spoken—it's all done with hand signals. You enter the game and immediately make a big bet. You stay until the count goes down and the game turns unfavorable. You then depart and wait to be called in to another favorable game by another of your counters. You have a tremendous advantage because your time is optimized, you are betting big only on high-count favorable situations, and you are playing with a joint bankroll that all members of the team kick into.

For example, suppose you had ten blackjack players, all playing with a $5000 bankroll. Now they form a team, pool their money, and play to a $50,000 bankroll. Accepted money-management theory says that a counter should not bet more than 2 percent of his or her total bankroll. **Two percent of $50,000, or $1000, is a lot more than 2 percent of $5000, or just $100.** This is called leverage, and it is the major advantage of Team Play.

It took the Nevada casinos awhile to catch on, and when they did, they instituted countermeasures and barred all suspected counters from play, including a man named Kenny Uston and his teams.

Kenny Uston, God rest his soul, learned this technique and perfected it to an extremely high degree of profitability. Kenny and his teams had been working Nevada until Resorts opened; then they "took over" the Candy Store in December 1978.

Ed Thorp, in the first edition of his book *Beat the Dealer*, conceived the idea of Team Play. This was back in 1961. It's amazing that the idea was not implemented until the mid-70s, some fifteen years later.

But Kenny and his teams made up for lost time. They took millions off the tables during the mid-to late-70s before they were barred from most Nevada casinos.

Team Play has advantages and disadvantages. I've told you about the major advantages of leverage and time optimization. But there is a disadvantage you must understand before you can use the tips on Team Play that will conclude this chapter. I will use some personal experiences to make my point.

The major problem with Team Play is honesty. How do you know if a team member is reporting his or her wins and losses honestly? On two of my own teams, I had the problem of a member skimming from the bankroll.

Kenny Uston used lie-detector tests for all his teams. And I did this for my Teams. But even if a polygraph gives you a favorable report, this is only at one point in time. What happens after the team is formed and money starts changing hands? On Kenny's teams, any member suspecting any other member of skimming could call for a polygraph at any time. But this became cumbersome and caused much distrust when it happened.

I also implemented more stringent money-control procedures through the team manager. My manager kept complete control of the bankroll. He coordinated and was involved in every team blackjack playing session. He would release the session bankroll prior to the session, monitor each team member's performance during the session (all members played in the same casino), and collect the money, including money won, if any, immediately after the session.

Money control became the accepted operational procedure and, from this point on, I had no more problems with skimming.

Is Team Play still effective? Yes. Although I personally have made much more money playing alone than with a team, I recognize the advantages to playing as a team if the problems cited above can be eliminated by using money control—a strong team manager is in charge and appropriate casino conditions are found.

And Team Play, contrary to popular opinion, does not have to involve playing with a joint bankroll. There are other advantages, such as scouting for winning tables and sharing this information, that can make team play very effective.

TIPS ON TEAM PLAY

As far as investment and finances are concerned, this is how a traditional blackjack team operates. A joint bankroll is formed from money invested by the players and perhaps nonplayers as well. The objective is to double the bank. When this objective is achieved, the profits are carved up as follows.

- 50 percent is divided up among the investors in proportion to how much each invested. For example, if one investor puts up half the bank, he or she gets half of this 50 percent piece of the bank.

- 25 percent is divided up among the players according to hours played. For example, if one player plays 10 percent of the total team hours played, he or she gets 10 percent of this slice of the profits, regardless of his or her winning percentage.

- 25 percent is divided up among the players according to money won. For example, if one player wins 40 percent of the total dollars won by the team, he or she gets 40 percent of this part of the profits.

Team Play techniques can also involve cooperation. Cooperation in finding playable tables. When you visit a casino with friends, consider working together! If you are card counters, each of you can scout for and find tables that meet your criteria and the criteria described in this book. If one of you is playing in a favorable game, you can signal your friend to enter the game.

I ran a Blackjack Training Academy for a number of years in the early 80s, and my students were much more comfortable using this approach to Team Play rather than the other technique. I called it "cooperative card counting." The approach is still viable under today's blackjack conditions.

Three players in one casino can monitor playing conditions much easier than one player. Think back to the last time you visited a casino with friends. What did you do? Probably went in your own direction after entering the casino and found and played at your own selected table. Then you met your friends later for dinner or a drink. Next time try cooperation. It's more fun and more effective!

The Nevada and Atlantic City casinos have curtailed, but not totally stopped, organized Team Play. But legalized casino gambling is expanding well beyond the boundaries of these two locations in the U.S. as noted earlier. In addition, Canada has legalized gambling, and blackjack is played in scores of foreign countries including most European countries and many countries in Asia.

Organized Team Play techniques can be applied to these games if you are prepared to make the investment of time and funds.

Many of the blackjack teams operating in the early 1980s used Shuffle-Tracking — one of the most powerful strategies to emerge from Research Pathway 1. We'll get to that in the next chapter.

Nine

AN ADVANCED BLACKJACK METHOD FROM RESEARCH PATHWAY 1: SHUFFLE-TRACKING

JUST WHAT IS SHUFFLE-TRACKING?

"Shuffle-Truck."

It was an early February morning in 1981 and I was practicing card-counting drills in my Blackjack Academy when I first heard this mentioned. Startled, I looked up. My friend Dick had walked in. His business was in the same office complex as my Academy, and one of his services was polygraph tests.

"Shuffle-Truck. Those are the only words I can mention," he went on. "I just polygraphed a blackjack team from Czechoslovakia. I can't tell you what the question and answers were because that's confidential. But the words 'Shuffle-truck' might give you a clue and some ideas to look into."

I thanked him. We chatted awhile and then he left.

These two words, "Shuffle-truck," were to start me on a year-long project that involved system development, hundreds of hours of successful personal play with the resulting winning system, and then the formation of a shuffle-tracking team.

I recognized the words right away because I was familiar with the concept. "Shuffle-truck" was German for "shuffle-track." The concept of remembering the locations of certain clumps of cards in the discard tray and then tracking them through the shuffle and cutting them into play (favorable clumps) or out of play (unfavorable clumps) had been mentioned in one of the many blackjack newsletters published at that time.

Up until now I hadn't thought too much about it. But this was different—a blackjack team using a shuffle-tracking technique. Now. In Atlantic City. I was missing out on something big and I had to find out what was going on.

I immediately initiated a dual course of action. I asked my wife and partner, Nancy, if she would find the team and set up a dinner meeting with the team leader. In the meantime, I started experimenting with the idea by dealing decks of shoes and watching what happened to clumps of cards as they moved from the discard tray, through various types of shuffles, and back into play.

I began to see the possibilities in a few short hours and had many ideas to discuss with the team leader, Vladimir, whom I met a week later.

By that time we were also hearing rumors about the huge wins the Czech team was taking out of the Atlantic City casinos. We had an interesting dinner with Vladimir, but I didn't learn much. His English was not too proficient and he really did not want to tell me all that much anyway. I don't blame him. It was obvious by the general tone of the conversation that his team was hugely successful. Its members had escaped from behind the Iron Curtain by learning to play winning blackjack with this shuffle-tracking technique. They were playing and winning in casinos all over the world. Of course they had come to Atlantic City when they heard about the great rules.

Remember that at this time, the casino pit bosses had no idea whatsoever of this devastating new method. It didn't look like card counting to them because players would bet big right off the top of a new shoe. At that time it was virtually undetectable.

After this meeting I continued to practice and began to develop some ideas for how to track the clumps. A few more weeks and my system was ready for a casino test.

HOW SHUFFLE-TRACKING WORKS

I would keep a high-low count (aces and ten-value cards $= -1$; two through six $= +1$; seven, eight, nine $= 0$) as the shoe was dealt out. At the end of each half-deck, I would mark the count, using the clock positions on a chip. For example, if the count was $+9$, meaning nine more low cards had been played than high cards, I would turn the face of the chip to the 9 o'clock position. Minus counts were handled the same way, but with the chip moved off-center to signify the minus. At the end of a six-deck shoe with four decks dealt out, I knew the content of each half-deck dealt — whether or not it was rich in extra high cards (favorable to the player) or rich in low cards (favorable to the dealer).

Now the dealer had to cooperate for the system to work. During the shuffle, if the dealer picked up one half-deck in each hand and then shuffled the two half-decks together, I knew the content of that deck. For example, assume that the dealer picked up a half-deck in his left hand with seven extra high cards and a half-deck in his right hand with six extra high cards. He shuffled these together and placed the resulting one-deck stack aside ready for the next shoe. I now knew that this one-deck stack contained thirteen extra high cards. This is very, very favorable to the player because of a much better chance of being dealt a blackjack, a standing hand of nineteen or twenty, or drawing a high card to a hand totaling ten or eleven with a doubled bet. Also, with a shoe rich in high cards, the dealer has a much better chance of breaking on a stiff hand (twelve–sixteen).

My objective was to cut this favorable clump into play. Suppose the favorable one-deck clump was one deck from the top of the newly shuffled six-deck stack. When the dealer handed me the cut card, I would cut one deck from the top and bet big into my favorable one-deck clump. Mathematically I might have as much as a 5 to 10 percent advantage when playing into these favorable clumps.

By the way, this example also works the other way. Suppose that the dealer picks up two half-decks to shuffle both containing a surplus of low cards. This is unfavorable to the player because the dealer, drawing last, will break much less often than normal. So an unfavorable one-deck clump is cut out of play. For the example above, if this one-deck clump is one deck from the top of the newly shuffled six-deck stack, the cut is *behind* the one-deck clump. In this way the unwanted one-deck clump is cut out of play.

Two problems immediately presented themselves in my initial casino testing.

The first involved controlling the cut card. If some other player cuts the newly shuffled stack, he may inadvertently cut your favorable clump out of play or your unfavorable clump into play. So control of the cut card was essential to make the strategy work. This was accomplished in one of two ways: (1) asking for the cut card from whomever the dealer had given it to; or (2) loading up the table with one or more known players or with a team and then signaling to them where the stack was to be cut.

Early in my shuffle-tracking play, I was forced to play off the cut card because I was playing by myself and could not always control the cut card. But this also worked out surprisingly well because if the clump(s) was in the wrong place, this in itself was good information and I could bet the shoe accordingly. For example, if my favorable clump was out of play, I would "flat" bet (make the same-size bet on each and every hand) the shoe, marking the half-decks and tracking the shuffle in preparation for the next shoe.

The second problem concerned the shuffle. Not all dealers picked one-half-deck clumps as they shuffled. Some picked quarter-decks. Some picked three-quarters of a deck. To make my tracking accurate, I had to mark the count of the cards dealt in clumps corresponding to their picks.

I perfected my shuffle-tracking method over the next few weeks and practiced marking and tracking for about four hours a day. I practiced for different types of shuffles and different-sized picks. I exchanged ideas with another shuffle-tracking team that Dick was part of. They taught me some simplified methods for marking the count such as using different-colored chips for signifying clumps of high and low cards.

I then recruited a number of my experienced graduates to play with me so I could signal the cuts to them and command total control of the blackjack game. I also played at the same table as Dick's team whenever the opportunity presented itself. These games proved invaluable to me because of "dual tracking." I was tracking, and Eddie, on Dick's team, was using the colored-chip method for tracking. Our cutting agreed most of the time, as did our bet sizes. This "confirmation" boosted both our confidence levels in our respective methods.

Playing with my recruited graduates and as an hoc member of Dick's team, I enjoyed consistent and heavy wins throughout 1981 and into 1982.

There were many successful tracking teams operational in 1981 and 1982: my own, the Czechoslovakian team, Dick's team, and a large team operating out of Brigantine, NJ, who apparently learned how to track from the Czech team. Most of the shuffle-tracking data in existence today originated in one form or another with one of these four teams.

The Atlantic City and Las Vegas casinos caught onto the technique in 1983 and changed their shuffles to make it much more difficult to track the clumps.

SHUFFLE-TRACKING IN TODAY'S GAME

Is shuffle-tracking a viable strategy today? Yes, under the proper conditions. You must learn to recognize the characteristics of a "trackable" shuffle, which are described later in this chapter.

Because elaborate shuffles are time-consuming and therefore costly, many casinos have reverted to the throwback shuffles. They have found that, since so few players can track shuffles, it is more profitable to maximize hands dealt and take their chances on the shuffle-trackers.

In the world of blackjack, playing conditions run in cycles. The casinos have a tradeoff decision to make in deciding which type of shuffle to employ. They counteracted shuffle-tracking with complicated and time-consuming shuffles that were impossible to track. But they eventually discovered that these shuffles were costing them money in terms of down time, time when the dealer was shuffling and the players were sitting at the table, not losing their money. So do casinos opt to simplify the shuffle, play more hands, maximize profits and take their chances with the shuffle-trackers? Or do they continue to employ the complicated and time-consuming shuffles? If you were a casino manager, what would you do? Very few players have even heard of shuffle-tracking; fewer still know how to track shuffles. Of those who know how to track, a small percentage knows enough to do it effectively as a viable moneymaking strategy. Casino managers have finally come to this conclusion and that is why shuffle-tracking is once again a viable strategy.

Is this strategy one that you should learn? Although shuffle-tracking is a complicated strategy, perhaps the most complicated strategy ever developed for winning at blackjack, it is used in today's game by many advanced players. You will have to decide after reading this chapter whether or not to incorporate shuffle-tracking into your repertoire of winning tools.

CHARACTERISTICS OF A TRACKABLE SHUFFLE

First of all, the game must be a shoe game; a single- or double-deck game cannot be tracked.

Then there are two prime characteristics that must be present to qualify a trackable game: the type of shuffle employed and the size of the dealer pick.

The ideal shuffle to track is a single shuffle with one-half-deck pick sizes; the dealer breaks the stack, assume six decks, into two three-deck piles and shuffles them one time through, "picking" about a half-deck in each hand as the shuffle process is performed.

An example of a shuffle that is difficult to track is the "double shuffle." If the stack is shuffled through more than one time, the game becomes much more difficult to track. In other words, if the dealer breaks the six decks into two stacks of three decks each, shuffles them together, builds up a new six-deck stack, and then repeats this process all over again, the game is probably not trackable and you should not waste your time in trying.

"Pick size" refers to the number of cards the dealer "picks" in each hand during the shuffle process. The ideal pick size is one-half deck. But you can track quarter-deck picks up to one-deck picks.

A Shuffle-Tracking Primer

Picture yourself sitting at the table, counting down the six-deck shoe. You have already noticed that the dealer picks up about three-quarters of a deck in each hand when shuffling. (See Learning Drill 10 in Chapter 18 for techniques for estimating deck size.) Starting with the top of the shoe, you are marking the count each ¾ (3Q) of a deck as the cards are dealt and the hands are played. Suppose the count of the first 3Q is −6. You place a chip on the table in front of you to the 6 o'clock position. You offset it to the left of a base chip to indicate a minus. Suppose the count of the next 3Q is +4. You place a chip in the 4 o'clock position on top of the prior chip and move it slightly to the right of center to indicate a plus.

You continue this counting and marking procedure through the six-deck shoe until you have a stack of six chips when the cut card is dealt, signaling the dealer that it is time to shuffle. Knowing the count at this spot in the deck, you add two more chips to mark the count of the undealt cards. (Note: Each of the six chips corresponds to one ¾-deck clump and add up to 4½ decks. For simplicity we have assumed the dealer deals 4½ decks before shuffling. The last two chips mark the undealt cards in the shoe.)

For example, if your end-of-shoe count is +6, you have six extra high cards in this last clump. But you must mark this count as −6 because this end-of-shoe clump is effectively dealt as the cards are taken out of the shoe and placed in the stack ready to be shuffled. If you don't understand why this end-of-shoe count of +6 is reversed to −6, imaging dealing out this last clump. If you deal it out, with the six extra high cards counting as −1, your count is −6. To simplify the process, remember to mark this last, undealt clump with two chips for the two 3Q-deck clumps; assume each clump is −3.

Figures 9-1, 9-2, and 9-3 illustrate this procedure of marking the count, profiling the discard tray, and mimicking the dealer's shuffle process with the chips that represent a clump of cards the size of the dealer's pick during the shuffle process.

There is a simpler version than marking the count with clock positions. Use different colored chips to mark a "high-card clump" or a "low-card clump." This method was originated by Dick's team, with Eddie providing much of the creative input.

Now what do you do? The stack of chips in front of you is a profile of the cards as they sit in the discard tray prior to the shuffle. You move your chips in the same pattern as the dealer moves the cards. If he breaks the six-deck stack into two piles, you break your stack of chips into two corresponding piles. As he picks up each 3Q deck to shuffle, you pick up two chips, one from each stack, combine them, and place them into the new stack in front of you in the same pattern the dealer places the two 3Q deck clumps in front of him as a new 1½ deck clump.

When the dealer finishes shuffling, your chip stack mirrors the new six-deck stack. If the cut is two decks from the end, so is yours; move the bottom two chips to the top of your stack.

CHART 1:
Top View of Chip Stack Used
to Mark Count of Card Clumps During
the Shuffle Process

Top Chip

-3 (3 o'clock position)

-2 (2 o'clock position)

+12 (Use different-colored chip to indicate 12 and 0)

-10 (10 o'clock position)

+1 (1 o'clock position)

-7 (Chip will be positioned to the left to indicate minus

— see sideview)

+3 (3 o'clock position)

+6 (6 o'clock position)

Bottom Chip

FIGURE 9-1. *Top view of chip stack used to mark count of card clumps during the shuffle process*

Now what does all this mean? It means that you know, within a half-deck to a deck, where the favorable clumps are and where the unfavorable clumps are in the next shoe. This is very, very powerful information and can provide you with a tremendous advantage over the dealer.

Suppose, for example, that you have cut a deck and a half to the bottom of the stack that you estimate contains fifteen extra low cards and aces as shown in Figure 9-3. This is equivalent to a count of

CHART 2:
Side View of Chip Stack

-3	H
-2	G
+12	F
-10	E
+1	D
-7	C
+3	B
+6	Clump A

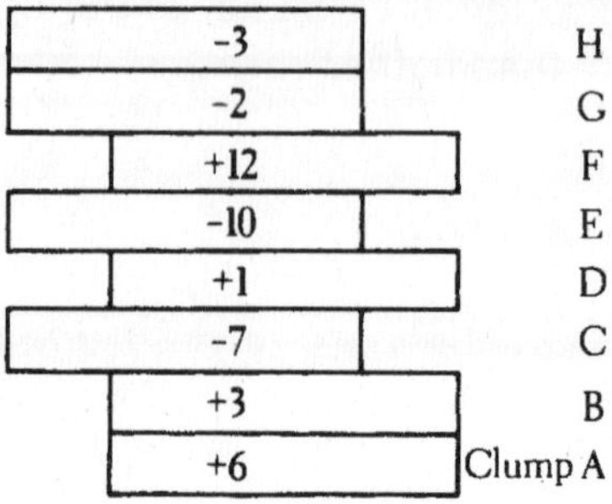

Note letters designating clumps
Each clump is $^3/_4$ (3Q) of 6 – deck stack

FIGURE 9-2. *Side view of chip stack*

+15 for the other 4½ decks and can be translated, using simple mathematics, to a player advantage of 5 percent for this shoe. Your betting strategy, then, is to bet big into these favorable clumps.

The reason you have the edge over the dealer is that high cards, tens and aces, are more valuable to the player than to the dealer. The player can double down (double his bet but draw one and only one more card) on a nine, ten, or eleven; the high card helps to win the double bet; the dealer, of course, cannot double down. High cards are more favorable on the player blackjack because of the 1½ to 1 payoff (for example, a $10 bet wins $15); the dealer collects only even money on his blackjack. And, of course, the extra tens work against the dealer when he must hit a stiff hand with a higher chance of breaking.

If you are interested in learning how to track shuffles, practice at home for at least fifty hours before trying the technique in the casino. Practice the procedure that I have described above. Cut your

CHART 3:
Using the Chip Stack to Mimic the Dealer Shuffle Process

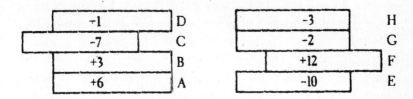

-1	D
-7	C
+3	B
+6	A

-3	H
-2	G
+12	F
-10	E

Dealer's first move

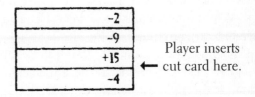

-2
-9
+15
-4

Player inserts ← cut card here.

The married clumps after the shuffle
Each shuffled deck is $3/4 + 3/4 = 1\frac{1}{2}$ decks

−4
−2
−9
+15

The stack after the cut card as it sits in the shoe ready for the next deal. Fifteen unfavorable low cards are cut out of play. Note that the first $4\frac{1}{2}$ decks contain 15 extra high cards (—).

FIGURE 9-3. *Using the chip stack to mimic the dealer shuffle process*

favorable clump into play or your unfavorable clump out of play. And then remove this clump from the stack and carefully examine it. How does it compare with what you predicted? If you predicted fifteen extra high cards, how many actual high cards are there? If the actual amount is within 25 to 33 percent of the predicted amount, you have taken the first step. But you are not ready for the casino yet! Will the technique I described above work in a casino? Put the book down now and ponder the next step that you must learn before risking your money in the casino. I never said shuffle-tracking would be easy!

The technique described above will work only if the dealer's pick size is ¾ of a deck. But what if the dealer picks a 0.5 deck or 0.6 deck? Will the technique work then? No. You have to modify your procedure to correspond to the dealer's pick size and adjust your chip manipulation to simulate the dealer's shuffle.

Before I take you inside my shuffle-tracking blackjack team operating at the time and show you exactly how it is done, let me make one suggestion about learning shuffle-tracking and then tell you a story that illustrates the tremendous power that it gives you over the casinos offering trackable shuffles.

First the suggestion: Read and study the team information when you are wide awake and mentally alert; skip ahead if you are in a relaxed mood right now and not in the mood for any heavy, intense reading. Come back to this data at another time when you feel ready to tackle it.

Now the story . . .

There is nothing like the feeling that comes from tracking a shuffle and knowing the "profile" of the next shoe — where the favorable and the unfavorable clumps are. One incident in particular stands out in my memory.

It was December 1981, near Christmas, and my son, Jim, was home for the holidays. We met one of my students, E., a restaurant owner from the Bronx who loved to play blackjack. He joined me every Wednesday night in Atlantic City for a blackjack play. I had taught Jim the signals for raising his bet and for playing his hand and had bankrolled him, telling him that he was playing to my full bankroll and I would give him 10 percent of the profits.

We were playing at the old Playboy Club, the plush Salon Prive, the third floor high-rollers casino, and I had tracked two high-card clumps and they combined beautifully as the dealer shuffled the decks. I got the cut this super-rich two-deck clump into play. Both E. and I made a five-unit bet ($250 for me) right off the top because we knew the high cards were right on top just waiting to be dealt. Jim bet $50, apparently missing my signal. All three of us won as the dealer broke. E. and I continued betting upward of $300 for the next several hands, winning most, with Jim finally nudging out a bet of five green chips ($125).

By this time I was getting upset with Jim, but I couldn't say too much at the table for fear of giving the game away. The next hand E. and I both bet $500 with Jim holding his bet at $100. Jim is dealt a beautiful blackjack with me pulling a stiff hand. Jim explodes with happiness with his $187.50 win, not even noticing my break and loss of $500 in his overall excitement. I found out what happened after the session. He had frozen at the thought of betting anything over $100! (the five green chips were even too much for him). We did end the session with a nice profit, but Jim did not get his 10 percent after that session. I flipped him an extra pink $2.50 chip that had resulted from one of my bad hands, probably the one in question, and said, "Let that be a lesson to you."

The blackjack hand taught him a valuable lesson when he understood that we lost $312.50 on the hand ($500 minus his $187.50 win) when we actually should have won $250 (he should have won $750 with a $500 bet; $750 minus my $500 loss should have been a $250 win).

JERRY PATTERSON'S SHUFFLE-TRACKING TEAM

This is information that I have never published before because of its sensitivity, and I think you will find it quite interesting and extremely useful. I will use Figures 9-4 and 9-5 to detail the technique.

Figure 9-4 illustrates a straight shuffle with six decks of cards. At the top third of Figure 9-4, a four-pick tracking procedure is detailed. On the left, the six decks appear as they would in the discard tray prior to the dealer's initiating the shuffle process. The ¾-deck clumps that are tracked, with thirty-nine cards per clump, are illustrated on the six decks, which are numbered one to six from bottom to top. Notice how every thirty-nine cards is marked off. The shaded areas represent the tracked areas and correspond to the chips in the chip stack illustrated in Figure 9-1. Be sure you understand this relationship. The chips in your chip stack represent values of the count for each clump of cards marked. In Figure 9-4 we are looking at a four-pick shuffle process of thirty-nine cards (3Q deck) per pick.

Still on Figure 9-4, now notice the middle part of the top third of the chart. The dealer has divided the six-deck stack into two equal piles with three decks in each pile. Notice how the tracked, shaded, 3Q deck clumps "marry" together as the top three decks in the right-hand figure in the top third of the chart. You have information about two 1½-deck clumps—the top two shaded areas marked "¼" and "case." Suppose "⅖" is your favorable clump, containing fifteen extra ten-value cards and aces. Where do you insert the cut card? Think a minute. The answer is at the bottom of this page.*

Now study the middle third of Figure 9-4, a five-pick shuffle process, and the bottom third, a six-pick shuffle process. In the middle third, do you understand why deck three (plus a small part of deck two), and deck six (plus a small part of deck five) are untracked? Because deck six, the unseen cards in the discard tray, marries with

---

*The cut card is inserted between "¼" and "⅖."

deck three. Because of the unseen cards, this information is not as useful, so there is no need to track deck three. The same reason holds for the six-pick process on the bottom third of Figure 9-4.

Figure 9-5 illustrates the shuffle-tracking procedure for the zone shuffle—a shuffle with clumps of cards spread around the table prior to the shuffle.

Notice the dealer's view in the upper left of Figure 9-5. This is how the two-deck stack appears from his or her vantage point prior to spreading the decks into "zones." Now, moving to the right, notice the six zones. The dealer has picked up the two three-deck stacks, set them down on the table in front of him, and spread them from the center of the table outward. (If you don't understand the process so far, arrange six decks of cards as shown and then go through the movements yourself.)

The bottom two upright rectangles on Figure 9-5 represent the six-deck stack, prior to spreading, with numbered half-decks, and show how these half-deck clumps look after the shuffle process. The dealer starts the shuffle process by picking half of deck six and half of deck one, shuffling them together, and then placing them onto the table in front of him. These two half-decks are represented as 1_2 and 6_2 to denote that they are the second half, or top half, of these two decks. The shuffled stack builds up as half-decks 2_5 are shuffled and placed on top of half-decks $1_2/6_2$, $3_2/4_2$ are shuffled and placed on top of $2_2/5_2$ and so forth.

The information in Figures 9-4 and 9-5 can be used in two ways. The first is to find a casino with a shuffle similar to the one analyzed in the figures in this chapter. And then practice your technique for that casino. The second is to use this data to devise your own shuffle-tracking procedure for the casino of your choice.

Important point: You must document the shuffle of your chosen casino carefully and perform the same detailed analysis shown in Figures 9-4 and 9-5. Be sure to notice the pick sizes and the movement of the cards as you document the shuffle. And then do all your analytical work and practice at home. (I am not suggesting you

CHART 4:
Shuffle-Tracking Procedure for Straight Shuffle

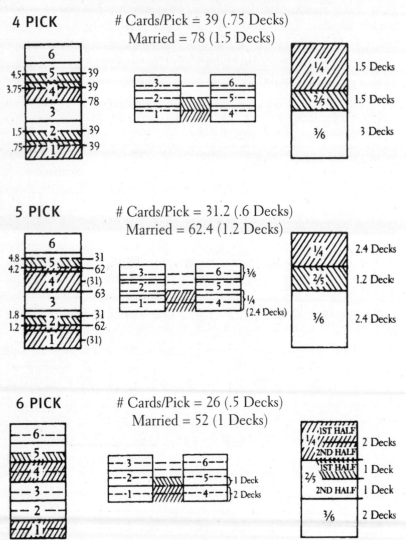

Decks 1 & 4 can be tracked as whole decks or as 4 half-decks
(Shaded areas are tracked areas)

FIGURE 9-4. *Shuffle-tracking procedure for straight shuffle*

CHART 5:
Shuffle-Tracking Procedure for Zone Shuffle

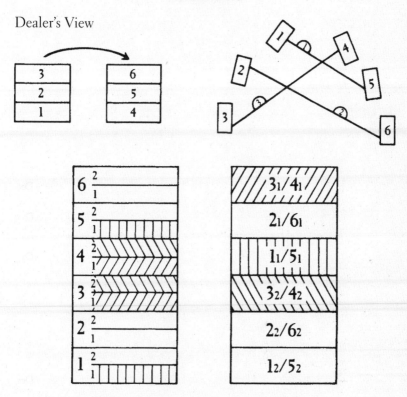

FIGURE 9-5. *Shuffle-tracking procedure for zone shuffle*

document the shuffle with a notepad in your hand; you must carefully observe the shuffle process, remembering the procedures, and then document it in an unobtrusive place.)

February 2000: An interesting footnote to the story about my son, Jim, under-betting that hand at the now long-defunct Playboy

Club (betting $125 when he should have bet $500). Jim did collect his profit from that session after all—he auctioned off on eBay the $2.50 chip I had thrown him for his share of the profits. He sold it for $149!

Ten

RESEARCH PATHWAY 2
RESULTS

So far, in my discussion of blackjack systems and methods, I have concentrated on what I defined as Research Pathway 1, or those winning methods based on card counting and other traditional techniques. But there is also Research Pathway 2—a major diversion from Pathway 1 and representing the premise on which this book is based. You were introduced to Research Pathway 2 in Chapter 7, in which the problems inherent in traditional card-counting methods were identified and the concept of biases caused by the nonrandom shuffle was introduced. In this chapter, more detail is presented about the Pathway 2 projects, including tips and tactics for short-term players—tips and tactics that you can use on your next trip to the casinos.

DEFINITION OF BIAS AND LIKE-CARD CLUMPING

Bias (from the *American Heritage Dictionary*): A preference or inclination that inhibits impartiality.

Biases result from the nonrandom shuffle (defined in Chapter 7) and cause like-card clumping.

Like-card clumping is generally the result of insufficient shuffling or methods intended to minimize the randomness of a shoe or deck. Such distribution — or lack of distribution — creates an unfavorable game for the skilled player. Sometimes the distribution creates clumps in near-sequential order, and this is why I do not recommend play for at least two hours after new cards are introduced in multiple-deck games.

An exaggerated example that illustrates the devastating consequences such clumping creates in eight-deck games would be a shoe in which all the tens and face cards — 128 in all — were placed at the top, followed by thirty-two nines, thirty-two eights, thirty-two sevens, thirty-two sixes, thirty-two fives, thirty-two fours, thirty-two threes, thirty-two deuces, and thirty-two aces.

Obviously, if you were to play this game, the area of the shoe loaded with tens and face cards would be a virtual standoff between you and the dealer. The rest of the game, however, would be devastating; you would lose the majority of your double down and pair-split hands and, statistically, the dealer would break less than 28 percent of the time, which is the average percentage.

Our purposes in studying biases and like-card clumping is very simple: if a series of events are nonrandom, then they must be predictable. But before we can get at a solution involving predictability, we must set forth the problem in more detail.

PROBLEMS CAUSED BY LIKE-CARD CLUMPING

When the Atlantic City casinos opened in 1978, two very favorable rules made the game attractive to card counters from around the planet: (1) the early surrender decision, and (2) the dealer was required to deal two-third's of a shoe before shuffling. Early surrender gave the player the right to surrender his hand and lose half the bet *before* the dealer checked for blackjack—an obvious advantage for the player since only half the bet was lost when the dealer drew a blackjack. Two-third's of a shoe was favorable for card counters since their advantage was based on the remaining cards in the shoe becoming rich in tens and aces. What a sweetheart deal it then became when a favorable shoe developed and the dealer was not allowed to shuffle it away. This all changed in 1981 when the casino management convinced the New Jersey Casino Control Commission to eliminate these two rules plus give them the right to bar card counters from play.

Kenny Uston, perhaps the most famous of all card counters and the one whose teams had capitalized on these two rules the most, sued the casinos over the barring issue. When he won his case in 1982, the game was changed forever because now the casinos were required to deal to everyone, including card counters. To reduce the threat of card counters, the casinos increased the number of decks from six to eight, and changed their wash and shuffle procedures. Their objective was to introduce card clumping into play by altering their wash and shuffle procedures.

The wash is the procedure casinos used when new decks are introduced into play. A new deck out of the box is ordered as follows: A to K; A to K; K to A; K to A. Each new deck starts with a natural clump because in its middle are eight high cards as follows: 10, J, Q, K, K, Q, J, 10. Subtle and sophisticated methods were used to introduce and perpetuate like-card clumping from the wash. One example is lining up two decks on the table surface, and then lining up another two decks right below the first two—two long lines of 104 cards, one above the other, then "squeezing" the two lines of cards together into one so that all the like-cards from one line are merged with like-cards of the other. You can imagine the fours, fives, and sixes being squeezed together into a like-card clump, but imagine what happens with that natural clump of high cards if the middle gets pulled together; the worst case would be sixteen ten-value cards, your most valuable cards, clumping up.

Even though these methods are not cheating, because the casinos have the right to wash and shuffle the cards any way they wish, they do subvert the card counting systems used to gain an advantage at blackjack. I wrote about this in my book *Break the Dealer*: "excessive clumping from inadequately washed cards can be encouraged and prolonged by sophisticated shuffling procedures." And that is exactly what happened; this was the major event that led to the initiation of Research Pathway 2.

Before we get into the details of Research Pathway 2, let's further your understanding of like-card clumping by showing its effect on card counting and then on basic strategy.

The Effect of Like-Card Clumping on Betting with the Count

Traditional blackjack card counting theory says bet up into a rising count. The card counter bets up into a rising count in anticipation of the extra high cards being dealt on the next round. But, often, they are not. A low-card clump, detrimental to the counter, advantageous for the dealer because of fewer breaks, produces more low cards out of the shoe and the card counter keeps losing. Ironically, when this happens, the counter is losing on the very kind of betting pattern that so many traditional blackjack authors have condemned: up-as-you lose betting. The counter will continue to raise his bet on losses when the count keeps increasing into a low-card clump.

The opposite phenomenon could also occur. The count goes negative and trends lower into negative territory; i.e., -4, -7, -10, etc. The counter is winning more hands than he is losing because more high cards are coming out (they count as -1, thereby leading to the negative count). But, the card counter is winning on minimum bets because he's not increasing his bet into the negative shoe.

The overall effect is the nullification of the card counters' theoretical advantage for all but the most skilled card counters, who have large bankrolls and can withstand the swings created by like-card clumping and play to the long-run. The large swings will kill the average counter by wiping out his or her bankroll. But betting with the count is not the traditional player's only problem. Clumping also adversely affects the basic strategy.

The Effect of Like-Card Clumping on Playing the Hands Using Basic Strategy

Let's take a hypothetical situation in which there are two players against a dealer involved in a game with excessive like-card clumping:

Player 1 is dealt five, four.

Player 2 is dealt seven, three.

The dealer's up-card is six.

Player 1 double downs and draws a six.

Player 2 double downs and draws a four.

The dealer turns over his bottom card and shows a five, and then draws a six and a four for twenty-one to wipe out the two players.

Let's look at the cards just played:

five, four, seven, three, six, four, six, five, six, four

Ten cards were played.

What's the most striking point about the sequence?

There wasn't a single ten or face card!

If tens and face cards are equally distributed, one out of about every three cards should be a ten or face card. This is one of the ways to detect like-card clumping. An abnormal clump of low cards or neutral cards probably means there is an abnormal clump of high cards elsewhere.

More importantly, the player's advantage on the double-down play was nullified! Keep this fact in mind because it suggests that basic strategy, the mathematical method for playing the hands, may not be effective in a clumped card game.

A low-card clump also affects the split decision. Consider:

The player is dealt six, six.

The dealer's up-card is six.

The player splits the sixes and draws another six so his hand now looks like this: six, six, six. He then splits again so is now playing three separate hands.

The player draws an eight to the first six, a ten to the second, and a five to the third, doubling down on the third hand and catching another five for a total of fourteen, sixteen, and fifteen.

The dealer, with an up-card of six, turns over the hole card of four, and then draws a four, five for a total of nineteen and wipes out the player's three hands and four bets.

Low-card clumps subvert the players' main advantage in Basic Strategy—doubling down, and splitting against dealer small up-cards. And if you can't win the double downs and splits, you are probably not going to win against this dealer.

Does this suggest we need to rethink our hand-playing decisions dictated by Basic Strategy? By all means yes, and we will get this consideration in Chapter 13.

WINNING METHODOLOGIES RESULTING FROM RESEARCH PATHWAY 2

Now let's look at the possibilities for winning in the clump card shoe games. Much has been done in Research Pathway 2.

Count Reversal

In the mid-80s I developed a Count Reversal System first published in the 1990s edition of this book, which recognizes that card clumping occurs in many shoe games and the count reflects this clump. For example, say the running count advances from zero to +15 over two to three hands. This is evidence of a clumpy shoe and means that an abundance of small cards, which count as +1, are being dealt; not good for the players, but good for the dealer, who hits last and can never break on hitting with a five or less showing as an up-card.

When the count reverses from a high point and begins to descend, this is the time to enter the game because the high cards, more favorable to the player, are being dealt.

The casinos have introduced countermeasures to reduce the effectiveness of the Count Reversal method so I have refined it and incorporated Count Reversal into a more sophisticated method called Count Profiles, described in Chapter 16.

Card Reading to Predict the Hole Card or the Next Card Out of the Shoe

If a phenomenon is not random, such as the shuffle in a multi-deck shoe game, it must be predictable. It was only a matter of time before astute Pathway 2 researchers would investigate the possibility of predicting the next card out of the shoe.

If you are sitting near or at third base with a hand of nine, two against a dealer up-card of seven for example, and notice these cards dealt to the other players' hands before you play your hand: five, two, three, six, would you double down? Basic Strategy says double. But what if you have determined that you are playing into a low-card clump? If you are, the next card will probably be small, thus nullifying your advantage and increasing the chances that you will lose this doubled hand.

Another example: Suppose the dealer shows a K and you are sitting at third base. Your second card is a six, and the first card dealt to first base after the dealer takes the hole card is a four. The next two cards dealt are also small—a four and a two. Could you assume that the hole card is also small? Do you see the possibilities here? The last four cards you've seen have been low cards: six, four, four, two. A low-card clump leading into and out of the dealer's hole card gives you the basis for predicting the hole card as small for this example.

Having shown you these two examples, I urge extreme caution if you attempt this technique because it does not work in every game. You have to qualify the game as a clump-card game, and mentally make these predictions, getting at least four of five of them correct before you employ the system in any game.

These examples are for illustrative purposes only. There is much more to card reading than watching card flows from one hand to the next. Unless you have time to research the technique on your own, you may wish to consider some advanced training such as that offered in my Blackjack Masters Course.

Dr. Steven Heller (now deceased) was the first to experiment with card reading in the mid-1980s. His research resulted in a two hundred-page manual called *Clump Card Blackjack*, or CCB. E. Clifton Davis's extensive research resulted in a method called New Blackjack, or NBJ. Further work was done by Ron Dibenedetto resulting in a method called Precision Blackjack, or PBJ. All of these researchers were extending the work Eddie Olsen and I had started back in 1982 with the development of the original target course and then both of us continuing our research but in separate directions beginning in 1985.

How to Use Like-Card Clumping for Table Departure

Since like-card clumping produces games with extreme plus counts (excessive low cards being dealt) or extreme minus counts (excessive high cards being dealt), this information can be used to make the table departure decision.

Depart when the count is an extreme minus, dealer-breaking activity subsides, and the game becomes dealer biased. Keep in mind that because of the nature of the shuffle in many shoe games, the distribution will not improve because of the shuffle. What you have done is to detect the beginning of deterioration.

If you are winning and the count is high, play into and through the high-card clump if it appears before the end of the shoe; keep in mind, however, that you are possibly playing in the last shoe of the game, departure is probably near.

While you are in a winning game where high-or low-card extremes are not evident, be sensitive to small-card clumping that you haven't observed before. Stay in the game, of course, while you are winning; but the observation of unusual clumping is the beginning of a reason to leave. Remember, the shuffle is not likely to improve or dissolve the clumping you have detected.

By being sensitive to like-card clumping, observant players can avoid losing situations. **A winning player understands that he must not only maximize his profits on winning tables, but also minimize his loss on losing tables.**

Oftentimes a winning session is saved by avoiding too many losing tables and keeping the profits won from winning tables.

Up-as-You-Lose Betting Progressions

Extensive research was performed in Research Pathway 2 on using three-level up-as-you-lose betting progressions in certain types of game situations, mainly to exploit neutral, back and forth games. In these types of games, the player rarely loses three hands in succession; the choice of the three-level, up-as-you-lose progression is betting against that happening.

For example, betting one unit on winning hands, but stepping up the bet to two units on the first loss and then four units after the second loss in succession. If the third hand is lost, the progression is terminated. Depending on game status and money won in this game, the termination could trigger a table departure. Any win in the progression recaptures the unit lost on the first hand and returns a one unit profit. This is a 1–2–4 progression.

This betting strategy has proven extremely successful in *qualified games*. Other, more aggressive progressions are used in strong games such as 1–3–5 and even a 1–3–7. Care should be taken that the game is qualified through at least one shoe.

The reader will find that up-as-you-lose betting progressions have been incorporated into the Count Profiles method described in Section 3.

Automatic Shuffling Machines

Although automatic shuffling machines have been around since the mid-1980s, research into methods for beating them did not begin until the mid-1990s, when the number used increased. First, some background.

Automatic card-shuffling machines are quite noticeable in the blackjack pits on the casino floor. They are big black boxes, positioned directly next to the blackjack dealer, at about tabletop height. They shuffle cards automatically; sort of a dealer's robotic assistant.

Professional automatic shuffling machines used in casinos come in several designs. Some shuffle single decks, some shuffle entire shoes (four, six, or eight decks) at a time, and others continuously shuffle, never stopping for a break.

With the most common types of machines, decks are shuffled a number of times. The machine then stops and waits for the dealer to put the newly shuffled cards back into play.

Procedurally, at the end of a shoe, the dealer takes all of the discard decks and places them into the machine for shuffling. At the same time, the machine has a newly shuffled shoe waiting for the dealer to place back immediately into play. There's no dealer shuffling downtime in the game. The dealer simply begins dealing the new shoe and the machine begins shuffling the old shoe. The machine usually finishes its shuffling well in advance of the dealer's need for a new shoe, so it stops and waits. To track the two shoes, different color cards are normally used. Typically there will be red decks and blue decks. One color is in play, while the other is in the machine.

In other designs, the machine continuously shuffles some number of decks, without stopping. Procedurally, the dealer deals from, and discards to, the machine while it is in constant shuffling motion. Theoretically, in this game, every card dealt is newly shuffled, coming from an infinite deck.

Automatic shuffling machines serve a twofold purpose. First, to improve efficiency. Second, to thwart blackjack card counters and shuffle trackers.

To improve efficiency, some manufacturers boast dramatic increases in the number of rounds dealt per unit of time using their automatic shuffling machines. Some claim increases of up to 40 percent in the number of hands dealt per hour. It stands to reason that casino managers would embrace these machines. Imagine, a 40 percent increase in hands dealt. That would directly equate to a 40 percent increase in table profits, right? Well, it turns out that, while casinos like them for use in some games, automatic shuffling machines produce something quite to the contrary. That is why we don't see them in more widespread use at blackjack tables. But more on that as we proceed through our discussion.

To thwart blackjack card counters, manufacturers boast that their machines "randomize" the cards to an extent where card distribution will never allow high-card or low-card clumps to occur. This simply means that card counts will always remain neutral, never giving a card counter his/her theoretical advantage play opportunity. Their machines also thwart players who employ shuffle-tracking play strategies. With the use of these machines, it is not possible to track shuffles. To these objectives, the card counting community generally concedes defeat. It appears that automatic shuffling machines work well to create something close to a truly random distribution of the cards, nullifying the effectiveness of most card counting play strategies, as well as shuffle tracking play strategies.

Automatic shuffling machines tend to produce games that are

significantly different from the typical dealer-biased games we see so often today. These machines tend to produce a near-random distribution of the cards and in these games, we find unique back and forth winning action between the house and the players. Neither side appears to have a significant upper hand. This is precisely the type of winning action we would expect to observe against a game in which the cards are randomly distributed and the players employ Basic Strategy. Remember that Basic Strategy, played perfectly, will decrease the house edge to less than 1 percent, *in a game where the cards are randomly distributed*. For this reason, we believe that these machines will not come into widespread use.

Automatic shuffling machines appear to give us a good, random distribution of the cards, and therefore they tend to produce an atypical game, which can be beaten with the appropriate advantage playing strategy; a strategy that utilizes the up-as-you-lose betting tactic discussed in the prior section.

A winning system for beating the automatic shuffling machines is described in Chapter 14.

Short-Term Money Management Strategies

Right up front in this book, I made the statement that few blackjack players ever play to the long term. Ergo, most players play to the short term. Short-term strategies are characterized by logical and defined table departure decisions.

Research Pathway 2 focused on three table departure tactics: stop-losses, stop-wins, and trailing stop-losses.

Stop-losses and stop-wins were introduced back in Chapter 4 on creating and managing a blackjack bankroll. The focus here is to use them for table departure to limit losses and preserve wins. The reader has learned in this chapter that card clumping causes dealer biases and dealer lead to dealer wins and player losses. Losses can be minimized by respecting a stop-loss table departure—three betting units for conservative players, up to ten units for more aggressive players.

Stop-wins also trigger a table departure. A fixed stop-win such as doubling your buy-in amount can be used, but trailing stop-losses are preferred. A trailing stop-loss is adjusted as winnings accumulate and prevent "give back," which is a common habit among less experienced blackjack players; i.e., giving back much or all of a table win. A simple rule can be employed such as never giving back more than three units (up to ten units) of a table win. As table winnings accumulate, segregate that portion you are willing to give back from the rest of your winnings. If your trailing stop-loss is six units, for example, this is the amount you would segregate from your winning chip stacks.

The trailing stop-loss is used in the Takedown and other winning strategies described in SECTION 3.

Results of Research Pathway 2

The major research projects in Pathway 2 proved conclusively what we had suspected—that many dealer-biased games occur in high-count situations. This happens because of card clumps produced by certain nonrandom shuffles. For example, low-card clumps can produce extreme high-count situations. The counter increases his bet in expectation that the missing high cards may appear: a twenty or blackjack or a face card to his doubled eleven. But because of extreme clumping, these high cards may not appear in this shoe. Or the high cards may be clumped, many showing up on the same round with most players being dealt twenties and the dealer pulling a twenty also. These high cards are now out of play and not randomly available to the player when one is needed.

We proved that like-card clumping can be devastating to a player. A major reason is that the dealer hits his hand last. The player will stand on a stiff hand, expecting the dealer to break. Playing into a low-card clump, the dealer makes hand after hand, breaking much less often than is mathematically expected.

But we also proved that like-card clumping can be favorable to the player. Many dealer-breaking tables occur on neutral to negative counts. The player can exploit these favorable games by up-as-you-lose betting progressions and money management tactics such as trailing stop-losses to preserve the win. The player can also exploit low-card clumps by hitting on stiff hands when basic strategy says stand; e.g., hitting a thirteen against a three up-card, for example, in anticipation of drawing a low or neutral to improve the hand.

Finally, because of the favorable results of Research Pathway 2, the neutral, back-and-forth games, choppy games, engendered by automatic shuffling machines, found in Internet casinos, and certain types of count profiles are now scouted for play instead of being avoided.

THE TARGET 21 METHOD

The key to winning is learning how to find the favorable player-biased or dealer-breaking games and learning how to avoid the dealer-biased or player-breaking games. The Target 21 Method was developed to do just that.

You don't have to analyze clumps or track shuffles to employ the Target 21 Method. The method itself will show you how to determine if the game is player-biased and whether or not you should get into the game (or leave the game if the table is deteriorating and the card bias is changing). The method is summarized in the next section.

Target 21 (*T*able, *R*esearch, *G*rading, and *E*valuation *T*echnique) is a proprietary blackjack-table selection method. It is the most significant blackjack tool resulting from Research Pathway 2 projects.

Target 21 identifies blackjack tables where the players have the advantage over the house. It works because of the nonrandom shuffle. Target 21 players learn to detect the highly favorable player-biased and dealer-breaking tables.

Blackjack research programs have used computers to study the game ever since card counting was invented in 1962. Tens of millions of hands have been played under ideal conditions with a perfect random shuffle. Unfortunately, as mentioned many times in this book, *a random shuffle does not exist in the real world of casino play* (except in those games where certain types of automatic shuffle machines are used). A random shuffle would be difficult for the casinos to implement in a game in which the dealer shuffles the cards since even a single-deck of cards must be shuffled seven or more times to assure random distribution of the cards.

Research on the effects of the nonrandom shuffle began in 1982. Much of this research took place inside the casino. By observing and recording thousands of hands, and by simulating thousands more, the project team, with the help of hundreds of my blackjack students, discovered the characteristics of winning and losing tables. This is what we call Target 21. It comprises twenty-one factors that the player uses to evaluate a table. These factors indicate whether or not the table is player-biased or dealer-biased. A player-biased table is one in which, because of favorable clumping, the players will win 50 percent or more of the hands. A dealer-biased table is one in which, because of unfavorable clumping, the dealer will win 50 percent or more of the hands.

One of the Target 21 factors is the chip tray. To understand how to use this factor, let's assume you walk into a casino and see four tables in front of you. At three of the tables the dealer's chip tray is full. At the fourth table there are two empty columns with no chips. Which table would you play? Certainly you would select the table with the missing chips because the players could have won them. But that is not enough by itself because that winning activity may have happened hours ago and the dealer may be ahead now. It could also mean that players have come to this table, bought chips, played for a while and then left the table, neither winning much nor losing much. But what if the missing chips were won recently by the players? If this is the case, we may have a player-biased game. Of course, this one clue alone is not enough to give you conclusive evidence that this is a player-biased table. The Target 21 player uses this factor, in conjunction with five or more of the other twenty-one factors, to decide whether or not this table is an investment opportunity.

(*Note: Since Target 21 is a proprietary method, I cannot disclose all twenty-one factors in this book. But I will be happy to send you a twelve-page newsletter describing the method in more detail. Use the information request card at the end of this book to contact me. On the other hand, I did decide to publish a proprietary method in this book that exploits short-term opportunities created by the non-random shuffle. In Section 3 I describe an exclusive method called "Takedown" for recognizing a Target 21 table, and for exploiting the short-term opportunities offered by this player-biased or dealer-breaking game.*)

You will find a detailed description of Target 21 in Section 5.

Eleven

CONCLUSIONS AND RECOMMENDATIONS REGARDING THE TWO RESEARCH PATHWAYS

To end my discussion on the evolution of blackjack systems and methods along two research pathways, I will pose a number of questions that you may be asking at this point in the book and use these to offer my conclusions and recommendations.

- Question 1: Does card counting work in today's multideck shoe game?

- Question 2: Can blackjack be beaten in today's environment?

- Question 3: Which winning strategy should I adopt?

- Question 4: Should I learn how to count cards or is there a more effective way to win, better suited for today's blackjack environment?

- Question 5: Should I learn how to win from a book, a home-study course, or go to a school?

QUESTION 1: DOES CARD COUNTING STILL WORK IN TODAY'S MULTIDECK SHOE GAME?

For traditional blackjack players, in the multideck shoe games, only for the long-term, and assuming that they have sufficient bankroll and time to play to the long-term. Most blackjack players simply do not play to the long-term.

In Stuart Perry's book, *Las Vegas Blackjack Diary*, reviewed in the next chapter, Perry describes a three-month period of intense card counting play in Las Vegas. The winnings his $20,000 bankroll generated, he complained at the end, did not reach expected value and his conclusion was that he had not played to the long-term.

In Barry Meadow's book, *Blackjack Autumn*, also reviewed in the next chapter, a similar conclusion was reached after Meadow's sixty-day journey through Nevada. His outcome was different than Perry's; he generated $21,000 in winnings from a starting bankroll of just $8,000. But, in the end, Meadow said: "I was lucky. I could just as easily have lost. I could leave tomorrow, play sixty more days, and wind up behind."

Did Perry and Meadow play to the long-term? Their conclusions seem to say otherwise. I will leave you with a rhetorical question: If a two-month or three-month duration of intense, daily, blackjack play, cannot generate a long-term sample, what can?

We have discussed the problem of card clumping as it relates to short-term play. Simply put, clumping wipes out the card counters' edge in many games by inverting the information generated by the count. Instead of an advantage, as the count may indicate, the counter is playing to a disadvantage as he or she bets up into a low-card clump.

Not only that, the counter is committing the very sin for which so many card-counting authors criticize the player who uses a non-count system: Just like many gamblers, he is betting up on successive losses.

There is another problem, however, which all but nullifies any potential theoretical advantage the short-term counter expects to re-alize: bankroll swings versus small advantage.

Consider the short-term card counter in his or her attempt to grind out profits using a card-counting system. First, the counter must contend with boredom because betting with the count is a waiting game.

It has been shown in many card-counting books that high bets make up fewer than 5 to 10 percent of the hands. So when those high-bet opportunities present themselves, the adrenaline starts flow-ing as the big bet is pushed out. On a loss, another big bet is placed as the count increases into a low-card clump, and there is more adrenaline.

If the counter is using a betting spread of twelve to one, which many traditional blackjack books recommend for the multideck shoe game, it is quite easy to lose forty units or more in a clumped shoe. This ratio between high bet and low bet is necessary to over-come the house edge and give the counter his 1 percent theoretical advantage.

But these swings in the counter's bankroll are devastating and in some instances catastrophic to a player with the standard bankroll of two hundred units. Many blackjack card counting authors rec-ommend bankrolls of two-hundred units, and, in my opinion, even a two hundred–unit roll is not safe in a heavily clumped shoe game. It is interesting to note, however, that books published late in the twentieth century, have upped this units-per-bankroll number con-siderably—Vancura in *Knock Out Blackjack* to one thousand units, and Ian Andersen is *Burning the Tables in Las Vegas* to as high as two thousand.

Kenny Uston writes about downswings in *Million Dollar Black-jack*:

> "... if you were to play and enjoy a 2 percent advantage on every hand (which is unrealistically optimistic), after 2,500 hands you

would have a 20 percent chance of losing. This statistic is continually borne out by our actual playing experiences . . ."

He then goes on to describe a twenty-two–day period *"in some of the most favorable games I've ever experienced. The interval included five days of playing only positive four-deck shoes at the Fremont (team play), five days of juicy single-deck game at the Dunes, and six days of playing only positive shoes at the Desert Inn."*

At the end of this period, betting optimally to his large bankroll and with the True Count, Kenny was down $35,000.

Now you have an understanding of why I asked you to remember those two bankroll divisor numbers back in Chapter 3; today's player, playing to the short-term, with the winning strategies in this book, can start with a bankroll one-fifth or even one-tenth the size of the traditional card-counters' bankroll.

Here, then, are my recommendations for the traditional card counter in confronting the realities of today's multideck shoe games:

1. Do not bet up with the count on successive losses as most other blackjack books recommend; set a rigid table stop-loss amount and adhere to it count or no count. Table departure is the best decision you can make under these losing conditions because it is quite possible that this same low-card clump may come back to whack you in the next shoe.

2. Consider some alternatives from this book on how to exploit those other 90 percent of the hands where the count does not indicate an increase in your bet.

3. Consider abandoning the count altogether in the multideck shoe games and choosing an alternative noncount method from this book (see Chapters 13 and 14).

4. Play the single- and double-deck games in which card counting results more closely approach the theoretical models. Use

a short-term strategy in these games. There are many such games in the Nevada casinos and many casinos in other locations also offer these games. Study the methods in Chapter 17 for possible use.

QUESTION 2: CAN BLACKJACK BE BEATEN IN TODAY'S ENVIRONMENT?

Yes, blackjack can still be beaten. But it is not as simple as it was in the eighties when blackjack players could learn a point-count system, a basic playing strategy, and money-management betting tactics.

You have to recognize two realities of today's game:

1. For reasons already discussed; i.e., the nonrandom shuffle engendered card clumping, the count does not always work. You must learn when to use a count system and when not to. I will teach you how to do this later in this book.

2. Even if the count would always work against today's game, the pit bosses have become very adept at spotting card counters by their betting patterns. In Atlantic City, where state regulation prohibits the casinos from barring gamblers, pit bosses can either restrict a player's betting spread (the ratio between a big bet when the count is high and a small bet when the count is low) or shuffle up (shuffle and restore the cards to a new deck or new shoe to effectively remove the player's advantage) on a player if his or her betting spread becomes too high. In Nevada, a person detected as a card counter or thought to be a card counter may be barred from play.

QUESTION 3: WHICH OVERALL STRATEGY SHOULD I ADOPT?

The decision on what strategy to adopt can be made with information you acquire from this book. I will help you make this decision. If you learn how to count, it should become one of a number of winning tactics you employ.

The first major decision you must make is, should you treat blackjack as a short-term or long-term game?

If you do decide to become or remain a traditional player and treat blackjack as a long-term game, I suggest that you seriously consider the recommendations given above in answer to Question 1, especially the one about playing the single- and double-deck games.

I will recommend to you the most effective card-counting system and teach you how to bet with the count; all the information you need is contained in Chapter 15—A Handbook of Card Counting Drills.

But if you decide to treat blackjack as a short-term game, as I do, I will teach you when card counting should be used and when it should not. Short-term players have many advantages that long-term, traditional card counters do not, mainly that time is on their side. They choose their times to play; they decide when to enter and leave a table, not accepting the fact that they must play a waiting game, not accepting the risks of playing in an unfavorable game. They choose their games with care; they understand when they are in a favorable shoe or favorable segment of a shoe.

I will teach both short-term counting and noncounting methods coming up in Section 3.

QUESTION 4: SHOULD I LEARN HOW TO COUNT CARDS OR IS THERE A MORE EFFECTIVE WAY TO WIN, BETTER SUITED FOR TODAY'S BLACKJACK ENVIRONMENT?

If you haven't yet learned how to count, I recommend postponing that decision until a later date for reasons already given in this chapter.

Study this book and first prove to yourself that what I have written about the problems of card counting in the shoe games are real. Start by reading Stuart Perry's *Las Vegas Blackjack Diary*, which I review in the next chapter. This book will give you an excellent idea of the realities of card counting in today's blackjack environment.

Get into the habit of observing blackjack games when you go to the casino, either while in the game or from behind the table. It is easy to spot card counters by their betting patterns. For example in a round of play featuring few tens and many small cards, watch the players' bets on the next round. There is a good chance that the one increasing his or her bet is a counter. Watch a few more hands to determine if the counter continues to bet up into a possible low-card clump. Note the results.

QUESTION 5: SHOULD I LEARN HOW TO WIN FROM A BOOK OR A HOME STUDY COURSE OR GO TO A SCHOOL?

In 1978, when I formed the Blackjack Clinic, there were only two other blackjack schools in the country. The success of my school (in its heyday I was graduating over one hundred students per month) encouraged competition, and it didn't take long for over twenty other blackjack schools to come into existence. Now there are few, if any, left that I am aware of. With so many schools in existence, there were not enough students to support them.

The best and most effective way to teach, I have found, is to combine a Home Study Course with classroom follow-up. I have been using this teaching approach since 1984. The student purchases the blackjack home study program, studies at his or her own pace with telephone and email access to my instructors for questions and consultation, and attends Question and Answer, Dialoging, and Networking Sessions in the major casino locations. Consult Section 5 for details.

Final Word: At this juncture, we have established your winning foundation and presented you with a description of blackjack systems developed along two research pathways.

Before we move you into the winning arena, let's conclude this section by discussing the classic blackjack books.

Twelve

THE CLASSIC BLACKJACK BOOKS

AN ABUNDANCE OF BLACKJACK BOOKS

In 1978, when the first edition of this book was self-published, it contained my review and comment on every blackjack book in existence at that time. The same was true in the 1980s edition. Then, with the opening of the Atlantic City casinos, the market for blackjack methods, information, and instruction increased dramatically throughout the 1980s. In the 1990s, with the passing of the Federal Indian Gaming Act and states and localities legalizing gaming to get in on the gravy train, the market for gambling information exploded. When the 1990s edition was published, there were around fifty blackjack books in print and many of them, mainly oriented to card-counting methods, were just a rehash of many others. So I selected twenty-seven for review and comment. Now, as this new millennium edition goes to press, there are close to two hundred blackjack books in print, an impossible number for even the most experienced blackjack player to confront, not to mention the beginning players.

This growing list presents a serious problem to the many new blackjack players who seek more information about how to win. How does a player new to the game confront this many titles and choose one or more books that may be useful to him or her? You can get an idea of the scope of this problem by going to the Amazon.com web site and entering the keyword *blackjack*. You will be confronted by close to two hundred titles as you scroll down the pages.

Regarding this morass of information, we are compelled to ask the question: Have there been that many breakthroughs in the game, that many new approaches to playing and winning, to justify this plethora of books published about just one casino game? My answer is a qualified no, and this conclusion is based on over twenty-five years as a player, author, system developer, instructor, and analytic observer. Most of these new books, and most books published over the last fifteen years of the twentieth century for that matter, contain rehashed data and, in my opinion, are not worth your time, let alone your money. However, there are some classic titles available that *are* worth your time and money.

CLASSIC BLACKJACK BOOKS

I am recognizing this list of classic blackjack books for: (1) having one or more outstanding attributes (which I will list); or (2) having had significant impact on the game; i.e., have contributed to changes to the game by the casinos or to changes in the players' playing methodologies; or (3) an interesting read and telling some great blackjack stories. Some that I list may be out of print, but, with the availability of the major book retailers online, the online web sites specializing in gambling books, and the rare bookstores online, these out-of-print books are accessible to any blackjack player who invests a little time to make the search. With two exceptions, they were all published before 1982. This year is significant and can be considered as the "timeline" in the evolution of blackjack systems and methods. There is no coincidence to the 1982 timeline, as that was the year that everything changed in the world of blackjack.

Nineteen eighty-two was the year Kenny Uston won his suit against Resorts, which prevented the Atlantic City casinos from barring card counters, the year that eight-deck games were introduced, the year the elaborate shuffles and washes began to clump up the multideck blackjack games and make card counting obsolete in these games for all but the long-term card counters. Nineteen eighty-two was the year that the Research Pathway 2 was undertaken. With two or three exceptions, these classics were all originally published in the "good old days" when card counting worked in the shoe game. So listing them and reviewing them is a fitting way to end our discussion of the evolution of blackjack systems and methods. By the way, although I believe the book you are reading now belongs on this list, I did not include it. I will leave that decision up to you, the reader.

Position 13: Wong, Stanford. *Professional Blackjack*. Pi Yee Press, 1994, paperback, $19.95. Originally published in 1978.

Reason for inclusion on the list: Back-counting method — playing only on positive counts; good book for traditional players wanting to use the high/low count to play the hands.

When this book was first published in 1977, it revolutionized the way card counting was employed to gain an advantage at the blackjack table. Prior to this book, the standard way to play was to sit down at a blackjack table, keep a running count of the cards, and make small bets when the count was low and the dealer had the advantage, and large bets when the count was high and the player had the advantage. Wong's book changed this standard card-counting procedure. His approach involved keeping a count behind the table without sitting down, and therefore without playing any hands disadvantageous to the player. This method came to be called "back-counting" or "Wonging it." The player entered the game only when he had the advantage, leaving once again when the count turned negative and favored the dealer. In this way, the player was making flat bets and not following the usual up-and-down betting patterns of the typical counter.

It took the casinos two or three years to catch onto this method and implement countermeasures. In many cases, the dealer is instructed to shuffle up or restrict the player's bet size to the table minimum until the shuffle. This countermeasure is usually taken only if a player is obviously standing behind the table, waiting for a high count to occur. In today's games, many casinos simply bar midshoe entry, which, essentially, eliminated the strategy and made it obsolete except for those traditional players who use the book as a reference for its many tables and matrices, keyed to the high/low count, showing how to play each blackjack hand according to the True Count.

Position 12: Meadow, Barry. *Blackjack Autumn — A True Tale of Life, Death, and Splitting Tens in Winnemucca,* Anaheim, CA: TR Publishing, 1999, hardback, $27.95.

Reason for inclusion on the list: The best description for what it's like to operate as a solo professional blackjack player.

Blackjack Autumn is a must read for any player who's ever considered playing blackjack for a living. Publisher of a monthly horseracing newsletter and a casual but skilled card counter for over twenty years, Barry Meadow puts together an $8000 bankroll, arranges to take sixty days off from his business, and heads for Nevada with the objective of playing in every casino in the state. Meadow wanders through casinos from Las Vegas northwest to Reno, stopping along the way in such out-of-the-way places as Beatty, Hawthorne, and then continuing on from Reno to Winnemucca (where he does split a pair of tens as the subtitle indicates) and then east to Wells, south to Ely, back south to "Glitzville," and then completing the circuit in Laughlin, having played in 192 casinos and won over $21,000. Meadow tells about the life in real terms: the huge swings in his bankroll, the loneliness of cheap motel rooms, the bad buffets, the heat from the pit bosses, the fear about getting barred from play and of getting rolled for his bankroll, fighting to get a good game and a decent betting spread, and the nagging question of "why am I doing this?"

Even if you have no inclination whatsoever to turn professional, I recommend strongly that you read this book.

Position 11: Perry, Stuart. *Las Vegas Blackjack Diary*, conjelco 1997, paperbound, $19.95.

Reason for inclusion on the list: The second best description for what it's like to operate as a solo professional blackjack player. I reviewed this book in my new edition of *Casino Gambling* published in February 2000. A different book, different objectives, different ending than *Blackjack Autumn*. But same conclusion—the life of a professional blackjack player is not a pleasant one. Backed by a $20,000 bankroll, Perry spent four months in Vegas playing professional blackjack. He played 231 hours and won $2303, about what you can make at a Burger King flipping hamburgers. Perry blamed his small win on bankroll fluctuations and the fact that he did not play to the "long run." Perry estimated that fifty thousand hands or more are needed to play to the long-run and "in decent games." I blamed his small win on the fact that he didn't play in enough single- and double-deck games where card counting can work "in decent games" as long as you don't get thrown out by pit bosses or "counter catchers." Which he did, by the way, at least four times.

Position 10: Canfield, Richard Albert. *Blackjack Your Way to Riches*, Secaucus, NJ: A Lyle Stuart published by Carol Publishing Group, 1998, paperbound, $14.95. Originally published in 1977.

Reason for inclusion on the list: Great blackjack stories.

I've met Richard Canfield only once, but that was *not* enough. Raconteur, former pit boss, and blackjack player, he is truly a character right out of Damon Runyon. His book discusses the usual run-of-the-mill topics of interest to traditional blackjack players: Basic Strategy, card counting, money management, how not to get barred from casinos—but with one important difference. He is an excellent writer, tells a great story, and has a marvelous sense of humor. His is the kind of book you pick up and cannot put down. Canfield organizes his book well and uses sidebars liberally. He's as comfortable as an old pair of slippers, and when you read the book, it's almost as if he's sitting across from you, telling you these stories in person. And the stories. He sprinkles them liberally throughout the book's pages as sidebars. Read the sidebars if nothing else.

Position 9: Humble, Lance, and Carl Cooper. *The World's Greatest Blackjack Book.* **Garden City, NY: Doubleday & Co., 1980. Revised edition, 1987, paperbound, $9.95.**

Reason for inclusion on the list: More good blackjack stories.

This is an excellent book for the traditional blackjack player. It covers the game from A to Z, with a thorough description of Basic Strategy and card counting. It touches on the psychological side of the game and makes the player aware that he must gain control of his emotions if he is to become a consistent winner. It contains Humble's heavily promoted, but effective Hi-Opt I card-counting system.

And the stories. There are some very interesting blackjack stories in this book. The most interesting are those about Lawrence Revere and his trips to Toronto (Lance Humble's home city) and joint play, with Lance and his friends, in the private games that Humble introduced him to—games that could be found in any big city in those days before the Atlantic City casinos opened. Chapter Nine, Blackjack Outside the Casino, makes the book a bargain at $11.95.

Position 8: Revere, Lawrence. *Playing Blackjack as a Business,* **Secaucus, NJ: Carol Publishing Group, 1976, paperbound, $16.95.**

Note: 1999 Edition (Replica Books) does not contain color charts of Basic Strategy; I recommend the older version above if you can find it.

Reason for inclusion on the list: First book with detailed data on single- and multi-level point-count systems.

This book was the card-counter's Bible for a number of years. Published originally in 1971, it contains beautiful Basic Strategy charts in color and descriptions of four of the counting systems Revere developed with the assistance of Julian Braun. I first read this book in 1977 when I was doing the research for the initial self-published edition of this book. I remember devouring Revere's book from cover to cover and being extremely impressed with the work he and Braun had done. The book still sells well to this day and its data on point-count systems is better, in many ways, than the book's successors, which have rehashed and juggled this data upside down and backward without really coming up with anything new. Lawrence Revere was a colorful character, a demanding instructor, a creative system developer, and a winning player. As a former pit boss and with many casino connections, he was active on both sides of the table. There have probably been more stories told about him than any other blackjack player. As noted above, you can find very interesting ones in Humble's *The World's Greatest Blackjack Book*.

Position 7: Roberts, Stanley (with Edward O. Thorp, Ph.D., Lance Humble, Julian Braun, Jerry Patterson, Arnold Snyder, Ken Uston, D. Howard Mitchell). *The Gambling Times Guide to Blackjack*, Gambling Times, Hollywood, CA, 1984, paperbound, $5.95.

Reason for inclusion on the list: The only book in print which features several of the notable blackjack authors of the 1970s and 1980s. When I first decided to make up this list, I knew this book should be on it for the reason cited above, but, not having read it or even opened it in several years, I had forgotten most of its contents. Then, when I went to retrieve it from my library, I found it missing—lent, long ago, to a student or instructor.

Since the book is out of print, I searched the Internet and found a copy on the Amazon.com zShops. I ordered the book for just $5 plus $5 shipping and handling.

What a pleasure it was to open this book, first published in 1984, and read the chapters by Thorp, Roberts, Braun, Humble, Uston, and others. Two stand out and offer all the reasons you need to search for this book and purchase a copy: Chapter 3 by Edward O. Thorp, Ph.D. on "The Principles of the Game and Why It Can Be Beaten" and Chapter 10 by Stanley Roberts on Cheating.

Thorp's chapter takes you back to the days right after he wrote his bestselling book, *Beat the Dealer*, (reviewed below) and relates some fascinating stories about the early winning players.

Roberts's Chapter 10 segment on dealer cheating, his pictures of deck stacking, dealer card manipulation, including peeking and "second carding," make extremely interesting reading. Even though this topic of dealer cheating is covered elsewhere, I believe Roberts's description and graphics makes this book unique.

Position 6: Braun, Julian H. *How to Play Winning Blackjack.* **Chicago: Data House Publishing Co., 1980, $12.95. Out of print, but sometimes available from the Gambler's Book Club in Las Vegas.**

Reason for inclusion on the list: Best description of Basic Strategy.

The book is classic and timeless. It not only defines Basic Strategy, but shows you graphically and in color why each hand is played the way it is. But the book is more than a treatise on Basic Strategy. Braun recognizes the value of discipline and the advantage to the player of departing a losing table. He also sensed that there were cycles in the game, and is the first author I know of to comment on their occurrence. He offers no method for exploiting them other than the generalities of betting up when you are winning and backing off when you start to lose. How do you know when these winning and losing cycles occur? "Develop that sixth sense," he advised. "Sensitivity is a developed skill." These words, although general in nature, gave me some of my reasons for doing research that ultimately led to the development of the Target 21 Method.

Position 5: Uston, Ken. *Million Dollar Blackjack.* Originally published in 1981 by SRS Enterprises.

Reason for inclusion on the list: Best description of team blackjack and Uston's stories on team blackjack.

Million Dollar Blackjack book is a veritable handbook of cardcounting techniques together with practice routines. It leads the reader on a step-by-step program for learning Basic Strategy for playing the hands, a simple Level I count and, for those up to it, Uston's Level III Advanced Point-Count System.

Uston gives excellent instruction on betting strategies, multiple- and single-deck play, and blackjack team methods. His chapters on front loading, "spooking," and cheating are fascinating.

But the best part of the book, in my opinion, are the chapters on his own teams: their formation, their operation, and their successes and failures.

Million Dollar Blackjack is the book read by over 90 percent of the players who call my gaming company for instruction. Even if you never learn how to count cards, it is must reading and belongs in your blackjack library. An interesting footnote to this review is that Uston may have been the first player to recognize card clumping and its effect on the player's chances of winning. He discusses a game he got into several years ago in which new cards were introduced into play.

To quote:

"As we began play, I couldn't believe how the cards were coming out. Seven of the first ten cards were 4s. Then, a batch of 3s came out, followed by a group of 6s; then, a clumping of 10s and aces. I kept track of the count, which soared astronomically, as more little cards came out. Staying at $25 minimum bets, I lost hand after hand."

What Uston is discussing here is a game with an insufficient wash and the devastating effects of like-card clumping.

Position 4: Uston, Ken with Rapoport, Roger. *The Big Player.* Originally published in 1977. Out of print.

This book is a nontechnical narration of Uston's original Team 1 and the team approach to winning blackjack. His plans in the early days of Atlantic City casinos were to make the book into a major motion picture. He had the connections with Frank Capra, Jr. and Dale Crase as producers, but for a number of reasons I am not fully aware of, could never get it done. At one point, I remember he became dissatisfied with the screen play and actually rewrote it himself. Later he was disappointed with the actor selected to play himself and told me that he was the only one who could play himself.

Read about his many capers in fooling the casinos into thinking he was just another losing high roller, and you will believe him as I did.

Position 3: Thorp, Edward O. *Beat the Dealer.* New York: Random House, 1962. Revised version, New York: Vintage Books, 1966, paperbound, $5.95.

Reason for inclusion on the list: First book to publish a card-counting method for casino blackjack.

This is the book that started blackjack on the road to becoming the most popular casino table game with the publication of the first card-counting method for beating the game. The original edition was published in 1962, and contained a strategy for counting tens and "others" (all other cards). This system turned out to be extremely difficult to use in casino play. Card counting for the masses never really caught on until the second edition of Thorp's book was published in 1966. This included Harvey Dubner's High-Low Point-Count System, with basic strategy variations calculated by Julian Braun.

There were many other winning tactics published in this remarkable book, including a method for counting aces and fives. But the most interesting of these tactics is the one that involves "end play." In the old days, the casinos dealt the deck right down to the bottom, dealing fifty-one of the fifty-two cards. A counter had a tremendous advantage near the end of the deck because he or she knew what was left to play.

If you buy this book, try to find a copy of the original hardbound edition published in 1962 by Random House. In the 1966 edition, the publisher had to cut some of the most interesting parts out of the original edition to make room for the section on the High-Low Point Count.

Position 2: Uston, Ken. *Two Books on Blackjack*. Originally published in 1979. Out of print, but copies can be found on the Internet.

Reason for inclusion on the list: (1) a veritable history of Atlantic City blackjack in 1979 when the "candy store" was open for business; (2) excellent instruction for recreational players; (3) great pictures of Kenny in his glory days.

Two Books On Blackjack is really two books in one: (1) an adventure book titled *One-Third of a Shoe*, and (2) an instruction book titled *How You Can Win at Blackjack in Atlantic City and Nevada*. The One-Third of a Shoe portion of this book is Kenny telling the day-by-day story of forming Team 5 and playing during these halcyon days (Teams 1–4 were described in his first book, *The Big Player*). He describes the problems of selecting and deciding on the Team Members, of deciding on the size of the bank and the bet size, and of the Team almost disintegrating before it even began play because of a personality clash.

He takes the reader along with him on a wild, nine-day ride — the wins, the losses, the bankroll swings, the first double of a $60,000 bank, the encounters with the casino bosses and the other teams, the media attention, and the inevitable day when the fun had to end ("Black Tuesday"). His Team 5 ended up with a win, after expenses, of about $145,000. And memories they will cherish for a lifetime (unfortunately Kenny's lifetime ended just seven short years later, he died of unknown causes).

But this history of Atlantic City blackjack is only part of this wonderful book. The other half is a how-to book containing instruction for learning Basic Strategy including flash cards, some interesting facts about card counting, and a discussion of some common misconceptions and commonly asked questions.

I was hanging out with Kenny Uston in the late 70s when *Two Books On Blackjack* was conceived, written, and published. If you would like to read some interesting stories about my experiences with this most famous blackjack player ever, I'll be happy to send you an article I wrote. See Section 5 for details. (Also ask about sources for where to find *Two Books On Blackjack*, and, if I'm aware of any, such as a cache of five hundred that turned up in the year 2000 at Leaf Press in San Diego, I'll give you the information.)

Position 1: Baldwin, Roger, Wilbert Cantey, Herb Maisel, and James P. McDermott *Playing Blackjack to Win: A New Strategy for the Game of 21.* The 92-page classic originally published in 1957. Out of print. A collectors' item.

Okay, so it's out of print and almost impossible to find, a true collectors' item. And probably very pricey if you can find one.

Playing Blackjack to Win was published in 1957 with a near-perfect Basic Strategy. This book is really the forerunner to all the card-counting studies and strategies that have since been published.

I worked with two of these four pioneers of blackjack back in the early 1960s in the aerospace industry. In fact, Will Cantey was my advisor on the project to develop the first computer simulation of casino blackjack. He gave me an autographed copy of *Playing Blackjack to Win*, I wish I had it today.

The last copy I heard of was Julien Braun's when he put it up for auction at, as I recall, a starting bid of $400.

If you would like to examine a copy of this "Holy Grail" of blackjack, visit the Special Collections Room at UNLV next time you are in Las Vegas. Barry Meadow did and, to quote him from *Blackjack Autumn*: "Holding it in my hands, I feel like the guy in the archives who got to caress the Rosetta Stone."

Section Three

WINNING STRATEGIES FOR TODAY'S PLAYER

Thirteen

TAKEDOWN: A 4-PHASED NONCOUNT STRATEGY FOR TODAY'S PLAYER

INTRODUCTION TO THE STRATEGY

If you have ever played blackjack in a casino, you may remember a table at which you could do no wrong, the dealer kept breaking and you won hand after hand. Afterward, you may have wondered, "If only I had known, I would have bet much more aggressively."

This is the chapter you have been waiting for. After reading it you "will know" because it describes a strategy for exploiting a winning table, a table where the nonrandom shuffle has caused a bias that favors the players. This strategy, called Takedown (a stock market slang term meaning "to take down" a profit, or sell and take profits), detects short-term opportunities and shows you how to profit from them.

Here I aim to teach you how to profit from a winning table when you find yourself in one, without counting cards! Many players think that a winning table happens by pure chance, that the dealer's breaking hand after hand and "dumping" money to the players is pure coincidence, that they were just lucky to be in the right place at the right time. Well, this last thought is right. They are lucky to be there when the dealer starts dumping. But winning tables don't always occur by chance. And when your table starts dumping, you should be prepared to take advantage of it.

THE FOUR PHASES OF TAKEDOWN

Takedown is comprised of four phases:

- Phase 1: Table Evaluation
- Phase 2: Buildup
- Phase 3: Score!
- Phase 4: Takedown

These phases are simple to define. Phase 1 occurs after you enter a game. Using small betting units, you *evaluate* the table for potential. If the game doesn't pass a simple test and meet your conditions, you either depart or continue in the game, not losing or winning much, waiting for the conditions to be met.

Your goal in Phase 2 is to *build up* a substantial win without risking a lot of money. The game has proved itself as player-biased; you are beating the dealer and winning units.

When you enter Phase 3 in this game, you have already locked up a percentage of a hefty win. With the remainder of the win, your goal is to *score*, to win a much larger amount in this game with no risk whatsoever! When your initial profit goal of Phase 3 is satisfied, you immediately enter Phase 4 and start *taking down* profits. You will learn to stay in the game with your win-lock increasing as profits accumulate. Once Phase 4 is entered, you are guaranteed a table departure with your pockets bulging with chips.

Let's get into the details. In the following paragraphs I will teach you how to recognize each phase and how to move from one phase to the next. It is important that the goals of each phase be met before ascending to the next.

Phase 1: Table Evaluation

A mistake that many blackjack players make is buying more chips than they should be prepared to lose at any one table. When you buy in for $100 or even $50 at a $5 table, it is easy to stay until you lose this amount. The average player doesn't have the discipline to leave a table with part of his buy-in still in front of him.

The rule on the buy-in amount is to buy in for a little more than your stop-loss. If your stop-loss is six units, *and it shouldn't be more*, buy in for ten units. This will cover a double or pair split should it occur on your last hand. But be prepared to pick up four units and walk should your stop-loss be triggered.

When you enter any blackjack table, don't be too quick to raise your bet. Evaluate the table for at least the first two to three hands. If you win two out of three, with the dealer breaking on at least one of these hands, proceed to Phase 2. If you lose two of three, take it easy. And play to a short stop-loss. Remember, play no more than six betting units, preferably a three-five betting-unit stop-loss. If you lose two of three hands followed by a series of alternating wins and losses (a "choppy game") without reaching your stop-loss, you will have to decide whether you want the action of playing the hands or whether to look for another table. If the choppy game continues for one-two shoes, use the up-as-you-lose strategy described in Chapter 16 or look for another table.

If the choppy pattern breaks, you start to win, and find yourself up three betting units, then proceed to Phase 2.

The trigger for entering Phase 2 is a win of three betting units.

Phase 2: Buildup

Buildup means a gradual increase or expansion. That is the purpose of this phase.

We build up our buy-in amount as the table starts to pay off. The rule for Phase 2 is to win three flat bets before raising your bet. A flat bet is betting the same amount on each hand. For example, betting $5 a hand, your goal is to win three of these $5 bets, or $15, before raising your bet according to the rules discussed below. Important point: It will usually take you more than three hands to win the three bets; I am not suggesting that you win three bets in succession. Using the same $5-a-hand betting example, if you play six hands and win four hands, you have won two bets, or $10 ($20 for the four hands won − $10 for the two hands lost = $10 total win). You have not yet realized your objective, $15. If you play seven hands and win five ($25), clearly you are ahead three bets (assuming no double downs or blackjacks). You have won $25 on your winning hands and lost $10 on your losing hands; you are up $15; your goal accomplished, you now proceed to the next betting level.

A betting level is defined as a specific number of betting units. Level 1 requires you to bet one unit. In the above example, our bet size was a one-unit bet of $5.

Betting level 2 requires you to bet two units, or $10 (I will continue to use $5 as a sample betting unit; you can substitute whatever your own betting unit is that you have defined from Chapter 4).

The Takedown Method consists of five betting levels: a one-unit bet at level 1; a two-unit bet at level 2; a three-unit bet at level 3; a four-unit bet at level 4 and a five-unit bet at level 5.

Obviously, you are increasing your bet by one unit at each level. Your goal at each betting level is to win three bets, or: $15 at level 1; $30 at level 2; $45 at level 3; $60 at level 4 and $75 at level 5.

You must ascend through these five betting levels before you proceed to Phase 3.

Figure 13-1 summarizes this betting strategy and also shows you your stop-loss for each betting level. Remember—your goal at each betting level is to win three bets. Notice I said *bets*, not *betting units*. As defined above, your bet increases by one unit at each level. To review once again:

Your bet size starts at $5 (or one unit). You flat-bet until you are ahead three bets and then increase your bet size by one unit through each betting level. The reason for this increase is because the game or player bias is getting stronger and stronger.

A series of three losing hands will abort this betting pattern. The chart shows your bet reduction on each of the three hands. If your stop-loss is triggered, you either leave the game (preferably) or revert to Phase 1 and start over.

The only question not answered in this table is what to do after you reduce your bet on a loss and then you win the next hand, i.e. bet $10, lose; bet $5, win. The answer is, you increase your bet by one unit back up to the size associated with this level. For example, you're in level 4 and betting four units, or $20. You lose; you bet $15 on the next hand. You win; you bet $20 on the next hand. You lose; you bet $15 on the next hand. You lose again; you bet $10 on the next hand. You win; you bet $15 on the next hand. You win again; you bet $20 on the next hand. Now you stay at $20 until you have won your three units and then move to level 5; five betting units, or $25.

Figure 13-1 shows the one weakness in this method—a choppy table. If you chop back and forth, you're winning the smaller bet and losing the bigger one. This is where you must respect your stop-loss and depart the table or revert to Phase 1.

Notice that when you complete the five levels, you have won a total of $225, or forty-five betting units. Now don't get too excited and rush out to play this system, because you won't accomplish all five levels that often. You will abort the pattern many times long before you get to level 5. But you will abort with a profit if you leave the table; if you stay, you may give some of your winnings back.

Notice that your stop-loss at each level never returns all your winnings to the casino; you always abort with a nice profit.

Question: Do you count a doubled win or loss, or a pair-split win or loss, as two wins or losses in totaling your three wins or three

CHART 6:
Takedown Phase 2 Betting Strategy

Betting Level	Bet Size	Win Goal	Stop Loss	Betting Sequence On Series of Losing Hands		
	No. of $5 Units	3 Bets				
1	1 ($5)	$15	$15	5	5	5
2	2 ($10)	$30	$20	10	5	5
3	3 ($15)	$45	$30	15	10	5
4	4 ($20)	$60	$45	20	15	10
5	5 ($25)	$75	$60	25	20	15

FIGURE 13-1: *TAKEDOWN Phase 2 Betting Strategy*

losses for each betting level? I suggest a conservative approach: Total a win as winning only one bet, but total a loss as a loss of two bets. In this way you will exit a game with your doubled profits in hand while not risking any more money at each betting level.

To summarize Phase 2: Ascend five betting levels and win forty-five betting units.

On those few occasions—and they will occur in strong, player-biased or dealer-breaking games—when you do reach the pinnacle at the end of the fifth level, you will have built up a nice little bankroll of forty-five units starting with a buy-in of ten units and a stop-loss of six units (as defined in Phase 1). Not bad. But this is just for starters. Now we go to Phase 3!

Phase 3: Score!

If you get this far, you are probably playing at a dealer-breaking table. Or you are playing at a very strong player-biased game. So get ready to play much more aggressively, but with just a fraction of your win: twenty units ($100). Put your buy-in amount plus the other twenty-five units in your pocket as a *win-lock*, that is money that is not to be touched in this game under any circumstances!

Using a Fibonacci Sequence (see below), you are going to bet up on each win if certain conditions are met.

THE FIBONACCI SEQUENCE

Leonardo Fibonacci lived in the Middle Ages and attained the distinction of becoming one of the most eminent mathematicians of his time. His greatest contribution to the world of numbers was the so-called Fibonacci Sequence. This series of numbers (one, two, three, five, eight, thirteen, etc.) came into existence through a recreational problem having to do with the production of a pair of rabbits over the course of a year. Most modern-day numbers crunchers are familiar with this scholar's work, including certain stock-market forecasters who employ the Elliot Wave Theory to predict movement in the stock market. Some forecasters believe that certain natural cycles that occur in the universe can be predicted to follow a Fibonacci pattern.

For our purposes we will use the sequence to determine our next bet size depending on the outcome of the hand, whether or not the dealer breaks and whether the hand was a double down or split-pairs hand.

Here are the rules:

First, notice that each number in the Fibonacci Sequence is computed by adding together the prior two numbers. Three is $1 + 2$. Five is $2 + 3$. Eight is $5 + 3$. Thirteen is $8 + 5$. And so forth. The series looks like this if extended out a few more terms: 1, 2, 3, 5, 8, 13, 21, 34, 55, 89, 144, 233, etc. For betting purposes, we express each of these numbers in units. Again using $5 as our betting unit, we bet one unit, or $5, to start.

On a win and a dealer break, we proceed to the next number in the Fibonacci Sequence and bet that in units: two units, or $10. Again on a win and a dealer break, we move up the sequence and bet three units, or $15. Now the betting becomes more aggressive as we move up to a five-unit bet ($25), an eight-unit bet ($40) and so forth.

If you get to Phase 3 in the Takedown Strategy, you are playing at a dealer-breaking table or "Home Run" table: a table exploding with profits, a dumping table. (I have heard some pit bosses refer to these tables as "dump trucks.") Use the Fibonacci Sequence and bet aggressively to exploit this very exciting situation.

By this time your adrenaline will be pumping wildly; be sure not to let this interfere with computing the correct-sized bet and following the specific betting conditions set forth below.

- Start with a one-unit bet ($5). If you win the hand and the dealer breaks, move to the next number in the sequence for your next bet. Or, if you win and the dealer does not break, bet the same amount. A double-down or split-pair win would override the dealer nonbreaking hand and allow you to move to the next number in the Fibonacci Sequence; i.e., you win a double-down hand, the dealer does not break, okay to move to the next number in the sequence.

- If you lose a hand, you move back two levels to get your next bet size; i.e., lose betting twenty-one units; next hand bet eight units. If you lose two hands in succession, revert to a one-unit bet. Or, if your bet is above three units and you lose a double-down or pair-split hand, you revert to a one-unit bet.

After starting with twenty of the forty-five units you won in Phase 2, your initial goal in Phase 3 is to win at least fifteen additional units. As soon as this is accomplished, you enter Phase 4. If you lose the twenty units, leave the table.

Question: When getting into the higher betting levels of the Fibonacci Sequence, should I ever consider deviating from the Basic

Strategy for playing the hands and not risk the additional units called for by a double down or pair split?

Yes, because the loss of a doubled hand can be devastating psychologically. Also, a loss can wipe out most or all of the profit won at lower levels. A safe rule is to double down or split pairs only if the dealer shows a low card (two–six), a potential breaking hand, but then if and only if you won the last hand. Remember, you are executing a short-term strategy and you are not obligated to follow a Basic Strategy that is based on long-run mathematics. (For a description of the Basic Strategy, refer to Chapter 3.) And be sure to refer to the risk-averse Basic Strategy for Takedown Players at the end of this chapter.

Phase 4: Takedown

Now you are looking to take down your profits and exit the table.

There is a very simple rule for table departure. This rule is great common sense; it is not original. I first read about it in one of Huey Mahl's columns in *The High Roller Sports Newsletter*. It is simply this: Do not give back more than one-third of your profits. So, if you are fifteen units ahead, your stop-loss is fixed at five units. (Remember, you don't enter Phase 4 until you are at least fifteen units ahead from your Phase 3 play.)

Suppose you win another eight units for a total of twenty-three ahead. Move your stop-loss up to seven or eight units.

This stop-loss money-control method is very easy to follow at the table. Simply divide your winnings from Phase 3 into three piles of chips. Keep the three piles equal sized. That is, as you win money, divide the chips equally among the three piles. After accomplishing your fifteen-unit win goal in Phase 3, your three piles start at five chips each. As you continue to win, the three piles grow in equal proportion, six chips per pile, seven chips per pile, and so forth.

Now suppose you go into a losing streak. Work off one pile only, not touching the other two. When that pile is gone, you're gone;

it's as simple as that. If you start winning again, build this pile up until it equals the size of the other two. Then they all start growing at the same rate again.

Question: Can you dip into one of the other two piles if you need chips to double down or split pairs as called for by Basic Strategy? No! Don't do it. Respect your win-lock. Remember, we are playing a short-term game. We are protecting our win at this table right now. We are not playing for the long run. Do not accept the axiom of the traditional player that says you must play Basic Strategy on each and every hand.

Final Question: I can already hear my aggressive readers thinking, "Why do I have to ascend through all five betting levels of Phase 2? Why not just ascend through three levels and then proceed to Phase 3, especially if the dealer is breaking frequently?" Okay, I'll give you three levels, but not two! And if you're conservative, stick with all five. You'll leave more tables with a profit.

PRACTICE FOR TAKEDOWN STRATEGY

You can practice computing the correct bet size and determining your stop-losses and stop-wins by having a spouse or friend deal you winning hands at home. The idea here is for your "dealer" to deal from six decks of cards, but deal with the cards faceup and "set up" your winning hands. Not every hand should be a win; instruct your dealer to deal you two winning hands out of three. I suggest practicing your Phase 2 bets, ascending through the five betting levels, locking up your twenty-five units (or more) and then practicing your Phase 3 bets with the twenty-unit bankroll won in Phase 2.

Practice setting up your three chip piles and entering Phase 4 as soon as you win fifteen units in Phase 3.

A RISK-AVERSE BASIC STRATEGY FOR TAKEDOWN PLAYERS

Multideck blackjack is a game of nonrandom shuffles and biases. I, my instructors, and my students have long recognized that today's game is not the game that was in place when the Basic Strategy was invented back in 1958 by Cantey, Baldwin, Maisel, and McDermott. Nor is it the game that was in place when Braun modified the Basic Strategy in the 1970s. All of the findings of blackjack's pioneers were based on a game that no longer exists—a random game created by a computer.

You have learned in this book that card clumping affects your chances of winning and losing each hand and therefore your chances of leaving each table a winner. Because of clumping and its effect on the player's hand, Basic Strategy is in drastic need of an overhaul.

I and my associates did it and the result is called Clump Card Strategy or CCS. CCS is a risk averse strategy. Many double and split plays are devastating to the player. If you look at the math of the original basic strategy, 25 percent of all doubles and splits yield less than a 1 percent gain. Clumping virtually eliminates this gain so when you double down or split on these plays for no real gain, you are courting disaster. There is no value, no gain, no edge. In fact, depending on the degree of clumping, you may be doubling up into a negative expectation.

So I am recommending that you become strongly disinclined or reluctant to make these plays—become risk averse!

CCS eliminates all doubles and splits that do not deliver a measurable advantage to the player. When entering Phase 2 of Takedown, you are, essentially, starting out even with the casino in using CCS. All doubles and splits listed below deliver a 10 percent player expectation of winning.

Here are the changes to the Basic Strategy for the six- and eight-deck shoe games assuming you can double after splitting, resplit pairs, and the dealer stands on soft seventeen.

1. Double Downs

For a hand totaling nine, double down on a dealer upcard of four–six, NOT three-six as Basic Strategy says.

For a hand totaling ten or eleven, double down on a dealer upcard of two–eight, NOT nine or ten as in Basic Strategy.

On a hand of A, five, double down on a dealer upcard of six only, NOT four, five as Basic Strategy says.

On A, six, double down on a dealer upcard of five and six, NOT three and four as in Basic Strategy.

On A, seven, double down on a dealer four, five, and six, NOT three as in basic strategy. Do not double down if your hand is A, two, A, three, and A, four.

2. Splits

Never split twos, threes, and fours.

Split sixes on a dealer upcard of five and six only, NOT three and four as basic strategy says.

Split eights on two-eight only, NOT always; hit a pair of eights on dealer upcards of nine, ten, A.

Split nines on four–six only, NOT two–nine except seven, i.e., do not split on two, three, seven, eight, or nine.

3. Hitting and Standing

If your hand totals thirteen, hit on an upcard of two instead of standing. For any A, seven or hand totaling soft eighteen, stand on dealer upcards of nine, ten, and A instead of hitting.

4. Surrender

If the casino allows surrender, follow this strategy:

Surrender sixteen against a dealer upcard of ten or Ace even if your hand is a pair of eights; do not split the eights as you would using basic strategy; surrender sixteen against a nine including a pair of eights;

Surrender fifteen against a ten or Ace including an eight, seven; do not hit the eight, seven as you would do using basic strategy.

CONCLUSION

In a typical weekend's play you will not find many tables that will take you through all four phases of the Takedown Strategy. You may not even find one. But . . . you will reap profits as you ascend through the betting levels of Phase 2, even if you depart the table on a stop-loss at any one of these five levels. And . . . when you do find the Home Run table, you will be ready to exploit it for sure!

Fourteen

A WINNING STRATEGY FOR THE AUTOMATIC SHUFFLING MACHINES

THE STORY BEHIND THE SYSTEM'S DEVELOPMENT

Several years ago, while I was teaching a class of blackjack students in Las Vegas, I was demonstrating in Caesars how to identify and exploit winning games. I worked with one small group from the class between 2:00 P.M. and 4:00 P.M. then a second group from 4:00 P.M. until 6:00 P.M. The casino was fairly crowded. It was a Saturday afternoon. About thirty-five blackjack tables were open for business and most of them were full, with five to seven players in each game.

My first small group and I made several passes through the casino looking for telltale signs of winning activity. We first looked at chip factors at all of the open tables. We looked for balance. We looked for unusual attention from the pit. We looked for all the signs. Pretty ordinary stuff in the day of a Target 21 player. But, on this afternoon, every time we toured the casino floor, my attention was drawn to a particular table. The game was full, seven players, four men, three women. All of the players were quite happy and conversing, even though it was clear that they were not associates of any sort. They each had an adequate stack of chips in front of them. Upon first glance, this game had several markings of a player-biased game and

I instructed my group of students to perform an observation drill to verify the value of the game. After watching the prescribed number of rounds, we decided that it was a neutral game, that the players and the house were playing even. We were looking for a player-biased game, in which the players were clearly winning over the house. So, we passed on the game. Again, all pretty normal stuff.

However, this table became more and more interesting as the afternoon progressed. Over the course of the four hours I observed this game, no players left it. The same seven players remained seated at the table for at least four hours. Most remarkably, at the end of each shoe, each player's chip stack was nearly equal to where it was at the beginning of the shoe. This game was the most even, back-and-forth game I had ever observed. Every player was playing even with the house, never losing more than a couple of hands in a row. Winning hands and losing hands were nearly even at the end of each shoe. It was no wonder the players in this game were so upbeat. In most typical games, average players are cleaned out in just a matter of a couple of shoes or less. These players were experiencing a game in which their buy-ins were staying intact for hours. Free beverages. Good conversation with friendly folks. No risk of losing money. Hey, most players could have some fun in a game like that.

Okay. What was happening? Why was this game so unusual?

Here's what I observed: Caesars was experimenting with an automatic shuffling machine at this table. The machine was producing a random distribution of the cards and the players were all using fairly consistent Basic Strategy. With these conditions it makes perfect sense that a solid, back-and-forth game would ensue. And the proof was in the results. The experience of this particular afternoon got my juices flowing. I immediately set out to confirm my conclusions and develop a strategy to exploit this type of game. I did both very quickly.

During trips to the Turning Stone casino in New York, Windsor in Canada, Atlantic City, the Gulf Coast, and a few more casinos in Las Vegas, I found more automatic shuffling machines in use and observed nearly identical performance no matter where I went. In one humorous case, I watched a pit boss at the Luxor casino in Las Vegas become increasingly frustrated as his automatic shuffling machine failed to produce profits at a table for several hours. He diddled with the machine's settings several times, but still got no satisfaction. Finally, at the end of a shoe, the pit boss instructed the dealer to step aside. He turned the machine off, took it out of service, and personally hand shuffled the decks. A couple of shoes later, the table turned dealer-biased, the players all left, and I quit my observation.

By the way, about a month after that enlightening Saturday afternoon session at Caesars, I returned to find the machine gone. In the years since then, I have visited Caesars many times, and haven't seen automatic shuffling machines in a blackjack game anywhere in their casinos. I have also found that many other casinos temporarily experiment with these machines in blackjack, until they discover their neutral properties. In most cases, they discontinue use of the machines, preferring the strong dealer-biased games produced by most hand-shuffling techniques.

Now let's get to the method.

THE WINNING METHOD TO BEAT AUTOMATIC SHUFFLING MACHINES

As soon as I verified that my observations in these games were accurate and reproducible, I put together a sensible advantage playing strategy to exploit them for profit. I used the strategy myself and experienced solid success. I then shared it with several players in the JPE Network. All of them reported the same solid success with the method and continue to profit with it consistently to this day. I call the method, Autotrack.

Let's take it again, a step at a time. I'm going to give you two options of play with Autotrack. The first is for conservative, risk-averse players. The second is for players with a higher risk tolerance and an unlimited supply of adrenaline.

The Conservative, Risk-Averse Option

Step 1: Locate a blackjack game using an automatic shuffling machine. The two-shoe (red/blue) type is preferable over the continuous shuffler.

Step 2: *Qualify* the game to be *consistently neutral* or *slightly player-biased*. You do this by watching at least half a shoe. During that half shoe, observe each player. No individual player should lose more than two rounds in a row *and* the overall number of losing hands should roughly equal the number of winning hands of each winning player. If these conditions are not satisfied, then do not enter the game. It does not qualify for Autotrack play.

Step 3: Verify that *Game Integrity* is near perfect. This means that the dealer should break about every three hands, players should make their double downs and splits, players hit to standing hands when they are supposed to (in accordance with Basic Strategy theory) and dealers break when they are supposed to (in accordance with Basic Strategy theory).

You will likely find that over half of the automatic shuffler games qualify.

Step 4: If the game qualifies, then enter with confidence and play the hands using Basic Strategy for all of your hit, stand, double-down, and split-play decisions.

Step 5: Bet each hand using a simple, flat betting approach. That means betting one unit each hand. Of course, you will bet extra units when double-down and split decisions dictate.

With this conservative, risk-averse approach, in qualified games, you will likely win two to three units profit per hour of play. You will need a thirty-unit session bankroll and can expect draw downs of only five to ten units.

Step 6: Continue play for as long as the game continues to qualify. If you see that players are beginning to lose a few units each shoe, or players are beginning to lose more than two hands in a row, then it is time to leave. The game is deteriorating. If you find yourself drawn down five units or more at any time in a single game, that is also a departure signal. Leave to find a better game.

The Aggressive, High-Risk Method

The first four steps are the same as the conservative option, so we pick up with Step 5.

Step 5: Follow this aggressive betting progression:

On your first hand, bet one unit.

If you win the first hand, bet one unit on the second hand.

If you lose the first hand, bet two units on the second hand.

If you win the second hand, bet one unit on the third hand.

If you lose the two unit bet on your second hand, bet four units on the third hand.

Continue this one-two-four betting pattern. Upon every win, revert to your starting one-unit bet.

If you should lose three hands in a row, leave the game. It no longer qualifies for play.

Very aggressive players may substitute a one-three-seven progression for this one-two-four progression for even greater profit potential (but with greater risk).

Using the one-two-four progression, in qualified games, you may expect to win five-ten units of profit each hour of play. You will need a sixty-unit session bankroll and can expect routine draw downs of twenty-five units.

Using the one-three-seven progression, in qualified games, you may expect to win ten-fifteen units of profit each hour of play. You will need a one hundred unit session bankroll and can expect routine draw downs of fifty units.

Step 6: Continue play for as long as the game continues to qualify. If you see that other players are beginning to lose a few units each shoe or other players are beginning to lose more than two hands in a row, then it is time to leave. If you begin to experience frequent two hands-in-a-row losses, then it is time to depart. The game is deteriorating. If, at any time, you should lose three hands in a row, leave the game immediately. This game no longer qualifies.

Special Considerations

- If you opt to use the aggressive betting progressions, you will experience many double-down and split decisions on your second or third hand, when you have your "big bets" on the table. Should you go for it and put more money on the table? I'll warn you now that it is gut-retching to double (or even triple) a seven-unit bet on a third-attempt play, especially after your confidence has been eroded with two losing hands in a row. My advice is this: Go conservative and don't double or split. It's too risky. If you lose the hand, you'll maintain a better frame of mind for the decision. If you win the hand, then all you've lost are the bonus units.

- With the conservative Autotrack flat betting approach, most of your profits will come from blackjacks, pair splits, and double-down bonuses, derived from your slight player-bias. Profits come slow but steady with this approach. Be patient.

- With the aggressive Autotrack progression betting approaches, your profits come fast and furious. Your draw downs also come fast and furious. It's a wild ride. Be cautious and work to maintain your discipline.

- With the aggressive Autotrack progression betting tactics, your profits come from the game's characteristic back-and-forth profile. You don't have to win a majority of the hands. You simply have to avoid losing three hands in a row. Using the one-three-seven progression, your risk exposure in any given game averages eleven units, and you gain one, two, or three units of profit for every round dealt depending on which hand you win (provided you do not lose three rounds in a row). To stay in consistent profits, you need to experience only one stretch of twelve rounds without losing three hands in a row for every three-in-a-row loss.

- Approach each *new, unqualified* shoe with due caution.

THE CONTINUOUS SHUFFLING MACHINES

The King Shuffler

In the late 1990s, Shuffle Master, Inc., a Las Vegas Company, invented a machine they call "The King," which allows dealers to deal from a continuously shuffled multideck shoe.

There are other continuous shufflers manufactured and marketed by other firms, but The King is the most popular and is growing in popularity as this book is written. The primary reason for the popularity of The King and other continuous shufflers is that they speed up the game, thus allowing more hands to be dealt per hour of play, equating to more profits for the casinos. The other reason, of course, is dealing a continuously "randomized" game with every card theoretically available for play at all times makes the game virtually uncountable by traditional means for card counters.

As of this writing in early 2001, there are about 650 Kings installed. According to the company, the orders are increasing not only in the United States but also internationally. Because The King's market penetration is growing, it will probably become the dominant machine in the automatic shuffler marketplace.

If you're wondering if the automatic shuffling machines will eventually replace all human shufflers, stop wondering. They won't. Too many players, especially the high rollers, just don't like them or don't trust what goes inside a box. The dealers don't like them, either. In this instance, the casinos will cater to the whims of their marketplace.

The Card Counting State-of-the-Art: "Latency of Redistribution of Cards"

Does The King spell the death knell of card counting in the multideck shoe games? Not according to a small group of card counters who are working with a theory called "latency of redistribution," as described by John May in his book *Get the Edge at Blackjack,* a book that represents the state-of-the-art in card counting systems aimed at beating the automatic shufflers.

In the older models of The King, cards were inserted into the back of the shuffle stacker and, it was discovered, did not come into play again for a predictable number of rounds. Knowing the value of those cards, the counter, according to May, could determine whether or not a player advantage existed; i.e., if the latent cards were low cards, valuable to the dealer, the counter would bet up with the knowledge that these cards were out of play, thus favoring the players for at least a few rounds.

In his book, May reports that a professional blackjack team exploited this flaw in some of the early models of The King, and scored big in a Las Vegas casino that had installed them.

Does "Latency of Redistribution" still work? Did a team of professional card counters really use it to score big against The King in a Las Vegas casino? We have no reason to doubt John May's story. Still a mystery remains. Why didn't any member of this team go after the big $100,000 prize that Shuffle Master, Inc. posted in early 2000 for any blackjack player who could devise a card counting method to beat The King? Their deadline was May 31, 2000. No one claimed the prize. Was it too small in comparison to what the team was making and anticipated making? Maybe one day the full story will be told.

Warning: If you purchase John May's book, be careful! One of his latency of redistribution methods is based on the false premise that the dealer reinserts the cards into The King as players bust their hands, not waiting until the end of the round. On the contrary, dealers often wait two or three rounds, or even until the machine signals them, before reinserting the dealt cards back into The King. Most, if not all, casinos using continuous shufflers require that the cards from one round of play be preserved in case of a player dispute that would require the dealer to display each player's hand to settle it. As you will see in the next section, we are quite interested in the size of the clump of cards that the dealer accumulates before inserting it back into the shuffler.

Research Findings and Winning Ideas

In conjunction with this revision of *Blackjack: A Winner's Handbook*, my network of instructors, players and I have analyzed a sample of The Kings and other, lesser-known brands that are in operation at the time of this writing. Some of them may, in fact, be beatable by doing some simple analysis of the card clumps as they are reinserted into the machine.

As an example of our ongoing research regarding automatic shuffling machines, I quote "007," one of my blackjack instructors, regarding his "peek" inside one the King Shufflers that was jamming on his recent Caribbean cruise and his subsequent observations of a King in his home casino outside Toronto.

I spent quite a few sessions at first base right beside the jamming machine with the top and side covers being frequently removed for service.

All the shuffling seemed to take place at the very back section of the machine (where the shuffle mechanics were) one-half-deck at a time. When there was a half-deck clump accumulated, it was situated at the top of the feeder, clamped off and moved down in sequence towards the bottom of the machine. The clumps were all in a straight

*line one above the other, and clumped separately on about a 20-
degree angle. This is where the card jamming was occurring.*

In another session at his home casino north of Toronto, Ontario,
007 comments:

*I observed the cards at the end of each round played as they were
returned from the discard tray into the machine for reshuffling. When
a half-deck clump was accumulated and shuffled, it was moved down
in sequence toward the bottom of the machine for redistribution and
no further shuffling was done. If it were not for the varying amount
of cards played per hand, it would be simple to predict when those
cards would return to play.*

*There were four decks used for a total of eight half-deck clumps. If
break-card-clumps (cards from the players' busted hands) are present,
they are reshuffled together and come back to perpetuate this player-
breaking activity thus destroying the basic strategy player.*

*I only observed for a few days and came to the conclusion that to
beat them it would take a combination of card reading skills in a
readable game and clump card play. I was successful using these
tactics winning over 100 units in just four table sessions using a three-
unit stop loss.*

*Unfortunately, the casino removed the machines due to customer
complaints. That ended my research for the time being. It was only a
short sampling, but I did spend many hours observing, and am convinced that the machines are beatable by the skilled player.*

007's observations seem to be confirmed by an article on Shuffle
Machines published in the *Casino Journal* (December 2000). A reference was made to a continuous shuffler not actually shuffling the
cards, but simply taking the discards and "rotating them around" to
eventually be selected for play again *without shuffling*.

007's findings are also supported by Ron Fitch, developer of the
Boris Blackjack Software.

Ron has acquired patent diagrams for all Shuffle Master machines and for the PRO shuffler and the Random Ejection Shuffler.

Using his software to simulate the shuffles, he claims to have demonstrated that the Shuffle Master I, II and BOX can be beaten under certain conditions.

On the other hand, his simulation of the Random Ejection Shuffler seems to validate that the machine produces random cards, but then, after further review, he finds that, like Shuffle Master BOX, many games appear random, only to clump up later, depending upon the intertwine factors selected for the last several shuffles.

Regarding The King, Ron says that it is a work in progress. He personally claims to have observed and played in many King games with modest success. Postings on his Blackjack Dealer Discussion Forum and a Clump Card Newsgroup confirm his preliminary findings that the King Shuffler produces clumped cards and therefore may be predictable and thus, beatable.

Controversies have abounded in the world of blackjack regarding randomness versus non-randomness ever since I introduced the Target 21 Method way back in 1982. Target 21 is based on the fact that blackjack shuffles produce a non-random game, thus predictable, which can be beaten by game analysis and table selection techniques. Now this same controversy is erupting in the automatic and continuous shuffling machine arena.

The scientific community supports my findings regarding non-randomness. If you're interested in this subject, I suggest you pick up a copy of *Chaos—Making A New Science* by James Gleick (Penguin Books, New York, 1988), a book that explains, in layman's terms, what non-randomness is all about. The new science of Chaos proves that nothing is really random, that there is order in any series of observable events. From the back cover:

This new science offers a way of seeing order and pattern where formerly only the random, the erratic, the unpredictable—in short, the chaotic—had been observed.

Conclusions

If you're interested in learning how to beat the continuous shuffling machines, observation is key. As 007 did, observe any machine and its mechanics that is being serviced at or near your table. Many of the older models are still in use and you might just find one with latency of redistribution without having to go through the complex analysis as described in John May's book.

Get into communication with the dealer and pit personnel and find out how many decks the machine is dealing and how old it is and what model it is. If you play one casino consistently, develop a file on the machines in your home area casinos. Try to find out when they are cleaned. We have had reports from casino personnel that dirty machines produce more predictable, player-biased games, than clean machines.

Observe the size of clumps the dealer reinserts back into the machines. Their size is an important factor in learning how to read the game that the machine is producing. Consider using a shuffle-tracking technique from Chapter 9 to track clumps that are especially favorable to you (rich in high cards) or the dealer (rich in low cards).

Our research on automatic shufflers, especially the King, is on-going. For an update report on finding, identifying and beating the Automatic Shuffling Machines, please contact me using contact information at the back of this book. Inquire about The Killer Progression Method, part of my Blackjack Masters Home Study Course. This is one of the most successful up-as-you-win progression methods I have used and marketed in my twenty-five plus years in the gaming instruction business. Properly used with game qualification, The Killer Progression will beat any multideck game — hand shuffled or machine shuffled.

Fifteen

A HANDBOOK OF CARD-COUNTING DRILLS

INTRODUCTION AND DEFINITIONS

In this chapter I will teach you how to count, using the High-Low Point-Count System, in both handheld and shoe games and in games where the cards are dealt faceup or facedown. Card counting is easy and, if you can add 1 + 1 and get 2, you should have no problem in developing this skill. Eleven copyrighted drills, from a Card Counting Home-Study Course I once sold for $295, are included to make learning easy and fun.

A brief lesson on card counting was included in Chapter 7, and I will pick up from where that lesson left off to prepare you to understand and learn the card-counting methods described in the next two chapters should you choose to do so.

You are starting off the top of a fresh deck or shoe with a count of zero and subtracting one for each face card, ten, or ace you see, adding one for each two, three, four, five, or six that you see and ignoring all neutral cards: seven, eight, nine. This is called the "running count" because it runs right through the deck, or shoe, from top to bottom.

The running count, however, doesn't give you sufficient information to make a betting decision, especially in the shoe game. Before we can use the running count, we must convert it to a True Count. The True Count is the running count divided by the number of decks left to play. (Note: Learning Drill 10 in this chapter teaches how to estimate the number of decks left to play.)

The True Count is more aptly defined as a "count per deck." To understand what this means, assume you have a running count of twelve with three decks left to play. Twelve divided by three yields a True Count, or count per deck, of four. The count per deck of four means that you have about four extra high cards distributed in each of the three decks left to play—a more accurate depiction of the value of those high cards. To be consistent, I will continue to use the term True Count to define this simple calculation.

To conclude this chapter, I will instruct you on how to use the True Count for betting purposes. Many advanced card-counting strategies use the True Count to play the hand, but this is too difficult to learn and totally unnecessary in today's blackjack environment.

ELEVEN DRILLS TO GET YOU READY FOR CASINO PLAY

Learning Drill 1: Card Familiarization

The purpose of this exercise is to familiarize you with the values of the cards assigned in the High-Low Point-Count System: Low cards are two–six and equal + 1; neutral cards are seven–nine and equal zero; high cards are tens face cards and aces equal −1.

Take a deck of cards and turn over one card at a time. Announce the value either out loud or silently, as you prefer. When you turn over a high card, which are counted as −1, say, "Mi 1"; a low card is just "1" with no prefix of +1, just assuming that the low cards are plus; and a neutral card is zero—just ignore these cards because they don't affect the count one way or the other.

This is not a *counting* drill. Do the exercise until you are completely comfortable in recognizing the value of each card.

Learning Drill 2: Single-card Deck Countdown

This is done the same as Drill 1, except you now keep a running count as you flip over the cards. Your count should start with zero and end with zero since the twenty high cards (−1) balance out the twenty low cards (+1) and, of course, the neutral cards count zero. As you count down the deck, think the count silently to yourself. When you see a neutral card, just repeat the count for the last card. And remember to use the prefix "mi" for all minus counts.

Since you are counting down a balanced deck equal to zero, you should know the value of the fifty-second card before you flip it over. For example, if your count is "mi 1," the last card must be a low card (+1) to bring the deck back to zero.

If you make a mistake with this last card, you have made an error. Do not shuffle! Count down the deck again and get the zero count.

Practice this drill until you can count as fast as you can turn over the cards—about thirty seconds for the entire deck.

But, you can do better than that! Can you count down a deck in twenty seconds? Fifteen? Ten? The record is eight seconds, by the gal that ran my shuffle-tracking team. Shoot for twelve if you're really serious about card counting.

Learning Drill 3:
Two-Card Pattern-Recognition Drill

You will quickly learn that it is easier to count cards if you recognize the six two-card combinations: the "mi 2" combination is any two high cards; the "mi 1" combination is one high and one neutral card; the zero combination is a high-low pair or any two neutral cards; the +1 combination is a low and a neutral card; and the +2 combination is any two low cards.

To learn these combinations, take a deck of cards and, instead of turning over one card at a time as in Drill 1, turn over two cards at a time and announce their value.

Go through the entire deck, announcing each two-card combination as you flip it over. Remember, this is a familiarization exercise so do not keep a running count.

Do this drill until you are completely comfortable with each two-card combination. It will prepare you to count in any blackjack game.

Learning Drill 4: Two-Card Deck Countdown

This drill is the same as Drill 2 except you are turning over two cards at a time instead of one. Start at the top with zero and keep a running count through the deck. Pause before turning over the last two-card combination. You should be able to accurately predict its value. If not, do not shuffle, and count down the same deck once again.

Initially, strive for accuracy and not speed. That will come with Drill 5.

Learning Drill 5: Deck Scan

After you master the first four drills, you may want to improve your card-counting speed. This drill is similar to Drills 2 and 4 except that you hold the deck in your hand and scan cards instead of turning cards over from the top of the facedown deck. Hold the deck in your left hand, faceup, and push cards from left to right off the top of the deck.

Initially, keep the count in two-card combinations as in Drill 4. As you become more adept, you will scan three-, four- and even five-card combinations.

With a little practice you will scan a deck in twenty seconds or even less. Do not try to break the world's record of nine seconds! There are better things to do with your time.

You can also do this drill by breaking a shuffled six-deck stack into about six piles. The size should be easy for you to pick up and scan. Set these six piles in front of you. Starting with the pile on the left, pick up each pile in turn and scan from left to right, then from the top of the pile to the bottom (reverse if you are left-handed). Carry your count from pile to pile until you finish. Your count should be zero. At the beginning of this drill you can set aside two–three cards. At the end of the drill you should be able to tell the count of the set-aside cards. For example, if your count at the completion of the scan is +3, your three cards set aside should be three high cards (−1, −1, −1) to bring your count back to zero.

In the beginning, your target for completing this drill is two minutes. If your goal is to become a serious card-counter, you should be able to scan six decks in 1:20 or less. I have seen professional players break one minute with this drill. My personal best is 1:09.

Learning Drill 6: Multicard Hand Drill

The purpose of this drill is to teach you to maintain the running count while making a hitting decision in a multicard hand (a hand with three or more cards). Multicard hands often present problems for neophyte card-counters.

To start, use two decks of cards to make up a special training deck composed of twenty-five cards, eight aces, and six neutral cards (put the other cards aside for the next drill). Shuffle up this special deck and deal yourself hands. In each hand, deal cards until you get a soft nineteen (a hand totaling nineteen with one ace counting as eleven or better, or hard seventeen (a hand with all aces counting as one) or better. With the twenty-five low cards, you will find that most hands will contain three cards or more.

As you deal the cards, total the value of your hand, make your hitting/standing decision and keep an accurate running count. At the end of each hand, set it aside for later review.

When you reach the end of your training deck, the count should be +17 (twenty-five low cards minus the eight aces are +17). If you have made an error, recount the hands that were played.

Learning Drill 7: Minus-Count Drill

Many neophyte players have difficulty counting on the minus side of the scale. This drill is to correct that difficulty.

Take the cards left from Drill 6 and shuffle them thoroughly. These cards have a value of −17 (as the cards used for Drill 6 were +17, the leftovers must equal −17 to balance the two decks to zero).

With this special deck, do a single-card countdown similar to Drill 3. Because of the unbalanced deck, most of your running count values will be on the minus side of the scale.

After you are comfortable in counting down the deck, practice keeping the count by dealing out three hands. Draw cards to each hand until it is seventeen or better. Keep a running count through all three hands. When you finish dealing to a set of three hands, push them aside and deal three more. Continue until you are finished with the deck, shuffle and repeat the drill.

Learning Drill 8: Faceup Blackjack Game Drill

In Atlantic City games where the dealer's first card is dealt faceup, start your count with this card and move clockwise around the table after the second card has been dealt to each player. You count the two-card combinations of which there are five: (1) two high cards are counted as −2, (2) one high card and one neutral card are counted as −1, (3) a high card and a low card or two neutral cards are counted as zero, (4) a low card and a neutral card are counted as +1, (5) and two low cards are counted as +2.

From this point on you count each card as it is dealt, including the dealer's hand. You carry this count forward from hand to hand until the end of the shoe, at which point you start over from zero.

The Faceup Game Drill is the practice routine for developing the skills necessary to count down the six-deck game. Deal out hands from a six-deck stack. Play the hands with perfect Basic Strategy. Keep a running count as you deal and play. Use chips and play one of the hands as your own. Make a bet with chips equal to the True Count. You can factor your own bankroll size into this drill if you wish. If your bankroll is $1,000, for example, each chip would be worth $10 if you use a bankroll divisor of one hundred or $5 for the more conservative divisor of two hundred.

This drill develops mental alertness and concentration. You are performing five activities simultaneously: dealing, playing the hands, keeping the count, computing the True Count, and making a betting decision. If you have trouble with the drill, approach it in a gradient fashion. Start by dealing and playing the hands. Then add the count when you feel comfortable with this gradient. The True Count and bet can come last.

Learning Drill 9:
Facedown Blackjack Game Drill

The counting procedure in a facedown game is quite different, and more difficult, than in the faceup game. You start by counting the dealer's up-card and then your hand. As the other players hit their hands, these cards are dealt faceup; count them as you see them. If a player breaks (his hand total exceeds twenty-one), he tosses his first two cards (those dealt facedown) faceup on the table. While the dealer verifies the break, you count these two cards. Any player wishing to double down or split pairs must turn over his two unexposed cards. Count these as they are turned. After all the players play their hands, count the dealer's cards as they are drawn, after counting the hole card. Then, as the dealer settles each bet with those players still in the game, he turns over each player's two unexposed cards so they lie on the table nearest the dealer. Count these cards as the dealer flips them over; remember, the two uncounted cards are always nearest the dealer.

You now have an updated count from this hand. Here is the drill for practicing this facedown card-counting procedure.

On a tabletop and with six decks of cards, deal out four player hands, facedown, and a dealer's hand, first card down, last card up. Deal the hands so that the dealer's is on top of your little practice semicircle and one hand, your own, is directly in front of you on the table.

Starting your running count with zero, count the dealer's up-card and then count your two cards.

Without looking at the other hands, deal them cards at random, faceup. You are simulating the play of these other players' hands. You don't care whether these hands are played correctly or not; this is for your counting experience. Count each of these cards as it is dealt, just as you would in a real game.

Now play out the dealer's hand, counting each card as it is dealt.

At this point, you simulate the settlement of bets by turning over each player's two unexposed cards, placing them faceup and positioned nearest the dealer's hand. Count them as you turn them over.

Push the cards from this hand aside and repeat this process, dealing out hands, until you reach the end of the six decks. Check your count against the remaining cards to make sure you get the zero count.

Learning Drill 10:
Remaining Deck Estimation Drill

Knowing the number of decks remaining to be dealt is required to compute an accurate True Count and for other reasons you will learn later in this chapter. Here is how to compute this number.

Purchase thirty decks of Bee brand playing cards. With twenty-three of the decks, create the stacks as shown below and tie them with rubber bands:

- Stack 1: 4½ decks

- Stack 2: 4 decks

- Stack 3: 3½ decks

- Stack 4: 3 decks

- Stack 5: 2½ decks

- Stack 6: 2 decks

- Stack 7: 1½ decks

- Stack 8: 1 deck

- Stack 9: ½

These are your models; learn to recognize the size of each of them. Now take six decks from the remaining 7½ and practice cutting stacks that equal the size of your models. Visualize the cards you cut as remaining in the discard tray. As you cut each stack and compare it with the appropriate model, mentally subtract the number from the number of decks in the game to compute the remaining decks. For example, if you cut a two-deck stack and there are six decks in the game, subtract two from six to compute remaining decks. If you cut a 3½-deck stack and there are eight decks in the game, subtract the 3½ from 8 to get 4½ remaining decks.

Do this drill until you are skilled in estimating decks played and remaining decks to the nearest quarter deck (thirteen cards). If your normal practice session is one hour, you should devote five to ten minutes to this drill.

Learning Drill 11:
True-count Computation Drill

There is an alternate method for computing the True Count than dividing running count by remaining decks. Instead of dividing by remaining decks, you multiply by the inverse of remaining decks. For example, if there are 5½ decks remaining in an eight-deck game, you divide the running count by 5½ to compute True Count. An easier method is to multiply by 0.2 (1 divided by 5½). Assume that fourteen is your running count. Now think of 14 divided by 5½. Did you get the number right away? Look how much easier it is to multiply 14 times 2 and get 2.8 (the 2 is really 0.2; you can add the decimal point afterward).

The multipliers are all worked out for you and are shown in Figure 15-1 (Multideck Shoe Game) and Figure 15-2 (Single-Deck Game). For this drill, memorize and practice the multipliers for the game you are playing. For instance, if you are playing mainly four-deck games, memorize the values of 3½ down to one deck. Use the table in Figure 15-1 to add the computation of the True Count to the deck estimating that you do in Drill 10.

Remaining Decks	Multiplier
7.5	0.15
7.0	0.15
6.5	0.15
6.0	0.15
5.5	0.2
5.0	0.2
4.5	0.2
4.0	0.25
3.5	0.3
3.0	0.3
2.5	0.4
2.0	0.5
1.5	0.7
1.0	1.0

FIGURE 15-1 *Remaining Deck Multiplier—*
Shoe Game

Cards Played	Multiplier
13	1.3
17	1.5
26	2.0
33	3.0
39	4.0

FIGURE 15-2 *Remaining Deck Multiplier—*
Single Deck Game

HOW TO BET WITH THE COUNT

Once you have learned to compute a True Count, betting with the count is easy. Just bet the True Count in units. For instance, if your betting unit is $10 (see Chapter 11 for how to compute betting units), and the True Count is four, your bet is four times $10 or $40. Do not bet more than six units on any one hand.

HOW TO PLAY YOUR HAND WITH THE COUNT

Unless you are considering becoming a semi-professional or professional player, with two exceptions, you should not waste your time learning complicated strategies for varying the Basic Strategy with the count.

For the majority of blackjack players, the only two hands in which you should use the count to vary your play are (1) player sixteen vs. a dealer up-card of ten and (2) any player hand vs. a dealer up-card of ace—the insurance decision.

The decision for sixteen vs. ten is simple: If the running count is any minus, hit your hand. If the running count is any plus, stand. If the running count is exactly zero, you can flip a coin—it really doesn't matter. This hand occurs quite frequently and, if you learn how to count, you should learn how to make this play.

The second decision—taking insurance—is a little more complicated. On the insurance decision, you are betting that the dealer has a blackjack, that he has a ten-value card in the hole. This is a good bet if the True Count is equal to or greater than three, and if you are not playing into a low-card clump.

If you are playing into a low-card clump, the running count will have increased very rapidly, for example from +6 to +11 in a four-player game. A simple rule for determining whether or not you are in a low-card clump is to remember how the running count increased over two successive hands. If the running count increases by more than the number of players in the game in each of the two hands, you may be in a low-card clump; do not take insurance.

Taking insurance in a facedown game is much more difficult because of the unseen cards.

When you take insurance in a facedown game (usually a single- or double-deck game), you need all the information you can get, right then, in the second or two that you have to make the decision. The problem is that you might have a very high running count or True Count, sufficient to take insurance, but there are many unseen cards on the table that will influence your count. To make a totally accurate insurance decision, you must adjust your count for as many of these unseen cards as you possibly can. Here's how.

First, observe the cards of the players' hands on either side of you. Adjust your running count accordingly. Now comes the hard part: you must deduce the other players' unseen cards.

If another player has tucked his two cards under his chips, that means he is standing and probably has a pat hand. Assume the count of this hand as -1. If a player takes insurance on a pat hand, you can assume he has a twenty and assign a count of -2. If a player is holding his two cards in his hand, you can assume he either has a stiff hand or a hitting hand and assign a count of zero. If a player insures this type of hand, he is probably holding ten or eleven and you can assign a value of $+1$. All of these deductions must be made very quickly and totaled up into your "temporary" running count; i.e., adding or subtracting these assumed hand-counts to the running count carried into this hand. If this "adjusted running count" is two or higher in a single-deck game, go ahead and take insurance; if it's three or higher in a double-deck game, take insurance.

In the facedown shoe game, this adjusted running count must be converted to a True Count using the above procedure. If the resulting "adjusted true count" is three or higher, take insurance.

After you finish this "adjusted running or true count" for insurance purposes, revert to the "real running count" by eliminating your "deduced counts" and counting the cards as they are seen.

Sixteen

COUNT PROFILES: HOW TO USE CARD COUNTING TO EXPLOIT LIKE-CARD CLUMPING

AUTHOR'S NOTES ABOUT SYSTEMS DESCRIBED IN THIS CHAPTER

Note 1: In the 1990s edition of this book, I described two methods for card counters: (1) Playing on the Run and (2) Count Reversal. Both of these methods required table entry a few rounds into the shoe. Many casinos now prohibit midshoe entry thus making these two systems obsolete in many casinos. I believe, however, that the Count Profiles System described in this chapter is a much more effective strategy than Playing on the Run or Count Reversal.

Note 2: The "count" referred to in this chapter is assumed to be the High/Low Count or: $2-6 = +1$; $7-9 = 0$; $10-A = -1$.

DEFINITION OF A COUNT PROFILE

The Count Profiling method described in this chapter is completely opposite to traditional card-counting theory. Traditional theory says bet up into a rising count. The counter bets up into a rising count in anticipation of the extra high cards being dealt on the next round. But, often, they are not. More low cards keep coming out of the shoe, detrimental to the counter, advantageous for the dealer because of fewer breaks, and the counter keeps losing.

Or the opposite phenomenon could occur. The count goes negative and trends lower into negative territory; i.e., −4, −7, −10, etc. The counter is winning more hands than he is losing because more high cards are coming out. But, he's winning on a minimum bet because he's not increasing his bet into the negative shoe.

The reason is like-card clumping, which was defined in Chapter 12. The shuffles are not random; the cards tend to clump up in shoe games.

We can exploit like-card-clumping by first profiling the shoe and then selecting a betting strategy to exploit that particular profile.

If you're a card counter, you can remember shoe games where the count went nowhere, staying within plus or minus a few points of zero for the entire shoe and never generating any favorable betting opportunities. And this went on for shoe after shoe and you began to wonder why you're wasting your time in such a game. This is a choppy or neutral count profile. It's caused by insufficient shuffling, a nonrandom shuffle, which does not mix up the cards enough to change the profile characteristic of choppiness.

Other shoes can exhibit other profiles: a count going high and never coming down, or the opposite—a count going negative and never rising above zero.

The ideal profile for a card counter is a rapidly rising count, but a count, which does not come down too fast. If a high count decreases quickly back to zero and then into the negative range, the tens and aces are also clumped, are dealt too quickly, and the counter's advantage evaporates before he is able to exploit it with a winning hand, or at least get a shot at a winning hand. But these shoes don't always happen. They are just one of many possible count profiles.

Count Profiles, in many cases, tend to persist from shoe to shoe because of insufficient shuffling causing like-card clumping.

The method described in this chapter is based on this phenomenon; it doesn't work in every game, but it will work in many games. You will learn in this chapter how to determine if a profile persists from one shoe to the next and, therefore, can be used for predictive purposes.

BREAK-CARD CLUMPS AND COUNT PROFILING

The number of players in the game influences the degree of unfavorable like-card clumps.

The main reason is the dealer pick-up procedure. When a player breaks, the dealer picks up his cards right away after the break and places them in the discard tray. A breaking hand is normally a stiff hand like K, six followed by another high card: K, six, J. These are called "break-card clumps," and their length *increases* in proportion to the number of players in the game; i.e., the more players in the game, the higher the probability of longer break-card clumps. For example, consider a full table with seven players with three of them breaking on this round. Your break-card clump could look like this: K, six, J, four, ten, nine, Q, two, K. These nine cards enter the discard tray in this order as the players break, the dealer picks up their cards and places them therein. At the end of this shoe, the nonrandom shuffle will, more than likely, perpetuate this unfavorable clump into the next shoe.

The ideal shoe game for the Count Profiles Method is one with three or four players.

Three or four players produce fewer break-card clumps going into the discard tray and that's why shoe games with three or four players yield a higher probability of winning with the Count Profiles Method.

COUNT REVERSALS

Count Profiles are characterized by Count Reversals; *a profile is defined by the number of Count Reversals in the shoe.* A Count Reversal is determined at the end of each round of play based on what the count was at the end of the prior round; e.g., at the end of round 1 we have a count of + 8; at the end of round 2, the count is + 12 — this is not a Count Reversal; if the count had been +3 at the end of round two; i.e., reversing from the high of +8, this is defined as a Count Reversal. Again, we measure from round to round.

Consider a choppy shoe with the count oscillating between −5 and + 5 for the entire shoe; this is many reversals in the fourteen to fifteen hands dealt in the six-deck shoe with four players in the game.

On the other hand, a shoe with a rapidly rising count or vice versa, does not generate many Count Reversals. For example, a count increasing to +11 over two or three rounds before reversing, and then rapidly falling to, say, −5 before reversing again, will not exhibit as many reversals as the choppy shoe described above.

The number of reversals is an indicator of the degree of like-card clumping in the shoe.

A shoe containing few reversals, by definition, has more like-card clumping than a shoe generating many reversals. Think about it — if low cards are clumped together, the count will increase quickly without reversing; the same for high cards except in the other direction.

The more reversals a shoe exhibits, the higher the probability of dealer breaking activity in that shoe.

In an oscillating or choppy shoe, the count reverses quite often, either above or below zero, or around zero, and this causes more dealer breaks. For example, if the count reverses on a high count, starting downward, there is a better chance the dealer is dealt a stiff hand; i.e., more low cards are dealt early in the round including the dealer's down card, then reversing to high cards with the dealer therefore having a higher probability of drawing a stiff hand, thus a good possibility of more breaks. It works the same on the negative side when a negative count reverses to positive—the dealer may get a high card in the hole with a higher probability of drawing a low card up on the Count Reversal.

THE COUNT REVERSAL FACTOR (CRF)

The CRF is defined as a ratio: The number of reversals divided by the number of rounds played in the shoe. Take an example of a game with four players, including yourself. Figuring about 2.8 cards per player and dealer per round, 5 hands times 2.8 is 14 cards played per round. In a six-deck game with two decks cut off, this is about fourteen to fifteen rounds per shoe. The ideal scene would be a Count Reversal in every round, or a CRF of one—fourteen reversals divided by fourteen rounds. But this happens only rarely. A CRF of 0.5 is more likely.

Before we can learn to exploit like-card clumping by using a Count Reversal Factor (CRF), we must see the same Count Profile continue into the second shoe. Then we gain some confidence in our ability to use the CRF for betting purposes.

To determine the CRF, you must keep track of hands played and Count Reversals as well as your traditional high-low count. The next section shows you how.

How to Keep Track of Number of Rounds Played and Number of Count Reversals

This can be done simply by using chips of two colors—red and white for instance. Use one chip for each round—a white one for no Count Reversal and a red one for a Count Reversal. Looking at your stack of chips will reveal the Count Reversal clearly. For example, if there are ten chips and six are red, your Count Reversal is six divided by ten or 0.6.

The only difficult part of this procedure is remembering the count at the end of the last round so that a Count Reversal can be determined. When you are extending your running count into the new round of play, you have to remember where you left off at the conclusion of the last round and then compare that with the count at the conclusion of the next round. If you are a counter, this should become automatic with practice—holding one count in your head while you extend that count into the new round. For a memory aid you could use the thumb and fingers of your left hand (or right if you are left-handed). Press the thumb against the tip of your forefinger for a count of one, your middle finger for a count of two, your third finger for a count of three, and your pinkie for a count of four. Now, bring your thumb down to the first crease or wrinkle in your forefinger for a count of five, then to the subsequent three fingers for a count of six, seven, and eight, to halfway between the first crease and the second crease for a count of nine through twelve, and to the second crease for a count of thirteen through sixteen. Go to near the bottom of each finger for a count of seventeen through twenty. Remembering whether the count is plus or minus, I will leave to your ingenuity.

Determining the Count Profile

Your first full shoe of the game is used to determine the Count Profile. For this first shoe, I recommend back counting without table entry or flat betting, with your attention focused on determining the Count Profile (unless you have confirmed a strong player-biased game or dealer-breaking game that Takedown, described in Chapter 13, may have identified).

The second shoe will tell the story—does the Count Profile repeat? Or are you noticing a different pattern of Count Reversals in your chip stack?

Remember that your CRF is computed by dividing the number of reversals by the number of rounds played. It shouldn't take you more than five rounds to confirm a repeating profile.

BETTING WITH THE CRF—METHOD 1 (BASIC)

As we explained in an earlier paragraph, *the more reversals a count profile exhibits, the higher the probability of a dealer break.* This frequent count reversal profile producing a high CRF is very powerful and, if persistent, delivers a strong player advantage. The betting methods to exploit it are simple but flexible. They boil down to: Exploit your advantage, increase your bet as long as the high CRF count profile persists.

Betting Tactic 1: Increasing Your Flat Bet on a High CRF

Increase your bet by flat betting two units for example. Continue flat betting as long as you do not lose three hands in succession, in which case you would revert to a one-unit bet. A high CRF can be easily determined by a quick glance at your chip stack profiling the CRF.

Betting Tactic 2: Increase Your Bet by Using a Simple Up-As-You-Lose Progression

Increase your bet from one unit to two units after a loss, and from two units to four after a second loss. On three successive losses, revert to a one-unit bet and redetermine the profile or leave the game. On any win, bet one unit on the next hand.

In a strong game, with the Count Profile persisting through multiple shoes, increase your betting progression to one-three-five or even one-three-seven instead of one-two-four betting a basic one unit on the first hand of the three-hand progression and then up to three units and seven units on successive losses.

For this simple up-as-you-lose betting tactic, you are winning one, two, or even three units for each three hands you play.

On three successive losses, revert to the flat betting tactic as described above.

Betting Tactic 3: Increasing Your Bet on a Win for High CRFs

You could also increase your bet as you win on persistent Count Profiles characterized by the high CRF, say from a flat bet of one unit to two units on the first win, to three units on second win, then back to two units regardless of the outcome on the third hand in the progression, then repeating the process and starting with a bet of one unit. This one-two-three up-as-you-win progression could be increased to one-three-five on persistently high CRF's in successive shoes.

I suggest a trailing stop-loss of five units for either reverting to a flat bet or table departure.

Betting with the CRF — Method 2 (Intermediate)

The difference between this intermediate method and the basic method is that the intermediate method covers all the CRF ranges, not just the high range as in the basic method.

Five CRF ranges (A to E) are defined as follows, with general betting suggestions keyed to each.

0.8 to 1.0	0.6 to 0.8	0.4 to 0.6	0.2 to 0.4	0 to 0.2
(A)	(B)	(C)	(D)	(E)
Aggressive	Moderate	Conservative	Flat	Flat to Reversal

Now let's discuss each betting range in turn, from A through E.

Betting Range A: Betting Range A, high CRF, is your most favorable because the dealer is more likely to break in this range. So, similar to Betting Tactic 3 above, your betting can be aggressive; e.g., if your betting unit is $10, you could increase it in this range by 50 percent and then, perhaps, a half-unit ($5) or a full unit ($10) up-as-you-win with a regression to your basic bet on a loss.

Betting Range B: For Betting Range B, I suggest starting with a one-unit bet, and then increasing a half-unit on successive wins, with a regression to one unit on a loss.

Betting Range C: For Betting Range C, I suggest starting with a one-unit bet ($10) and then regressing a half-unit on a loss if you are playing in a $5 minimum game. Don't increase in this range unless you see the Count Reversal Factor move into the A Range over the first eight rounds of play.

For Betting Ranges C and D (heavy clumping), I suggest flat betting one-half or one unit and waiting for a count reversal, from a high plus count downward, before increasing your bet. If the count reverses, and the tens begin to show, increase your bet a half-unit or one unit on successive wins and no count reversal.

Always reconfirm your Count Profile on each successive shoe and respect your stop-loss for reverting to a one-unit, flat bet or table departure.

Now let's get into some more complicated, advanced methods for using the Count Reversal Factor for betting.

ADVANCED BETTING TACTICS KEYED TO THE CRF

This method is complex and therefore suited only for the serious player or the experienced card counter.

Before I give you specific betting recommendations, I need to define another type of information you may wish to track with your chip stack showing Count Reversals and hands played: dealer breaks.

Track dealer breaks for each round by offsetting the chip representing the hands played, either red or white, to the right.

If you want to go all the way on tracking useful information, you could also track winning versus losing rounds of play. A winning round is when half or more of the players win their hands. A losing round is when more than half of the players lose their hands. Position your chip representing the round played straight up for a winning round; i.e., the casino name and the denomination at the 12 o'clock position; for a losing round just the opposite—turn it to the 6 o'clock position. To make your chip stack easy to read, offset the chip representing a winning round up slightly from the chip it is resting on, or down slightly for a losing round.

This chip placement scheme to profile the shoe may sound a little complicated, but when you think about it, it is actually quite simple. To start, you are picking up just one chip—either red or white to signify whether or not the round contained a Count Reversal. Second, you orient the chip up or down to signify the winning or losing round. Third, you place it on the stack offset to the right to signify the dealer break.

It will, however, take some practice to use the information thus obtained. First you have to quickly estimate the Count Reversal Factor by glancing at your stack. Then, for the prior four rounds of play, determine if the dealer breaks are positive (two or more breaks) and if winning rounds are positive (two or more winning rounds).

Let's look at each of the five CRF ranges (A, B, C, D, E), compared to the prior four rounds of play, to define our bet for the next round of play. Please note that the table in Figure 16-1 below represents an aggressive betting strategy. Less aggressive tactics are suggested in a later paragraph.

In examining Figure 16-1, you must decide which information to track. Columns 1 and 2 are included for those readers who wish to track one or the other of dealer breaks or winning/losing rounds. If you track both, just use the last three columns.

	dealer breaks positive	winning rounds positive	both positive	one positive/ one negative	both negative
A	up a unit	up a unit	up 2 units	up a unit on Last round win	one unit
B	up a unit on win or same	up a unit on win or same	up 2 units on win or same	one unit or up a unit on reversal	one unit
C	up a unit on 2 wins or same	up a unit on 2 wins or same	up 2 units on 2 wins or same	1 unit or up a unit on reversal & win	one unit
D	same as last hand or -1 on loss	same as last hand or -1 loss	same as last hand or down a unit on loss	1 unit or up a unit on reversal & 2 wins	1 unit on reversal
E	down a unit	down a unit	same or down 1 unit on loss	1 unit	1 unit

FIGURE 16-1: *Betting Tactics Keyed to Multiple Variables*

Recommendation: Start by proving to yourself the Count Profiles exist and perpetuate from shoe to shoe in many games. Then move into the basic betting tactics for the many "choppy" count profiles you detect. A good way to practice identifying choppy games is to practice on the Internet Casinos in the "free play" mode. You won't be able to segregate one shoe from the next, but you can learn to detect choppy games in many of the Internet casinos' random-number-generated games (see Chapter 21 for details).

As you get more experience in tracking count profiles, move to the intermediate betting tactics. If you're really serious, consider using the advanced betting methods.

Question: Won't I get too much casino attention by the chip

stacks you recommend keeping for tracking purposes? No. If anyone asks, tell them the truth, that you are counting your wins and losses and dealer breaks so you can decide how much to bet.

SUMMARY OF COUNT PROFILE BETTING TACTICS

Basic Method 1: Three betting tactics keyed to High CRFs

- Betting Tactic 1: Increase flat bet
- Betting Tactic 2: Up-as-you-lose to three levels
- Betting Tactic 3: Up-as-you-win to three levels

Intermediate Method 2: Betting tactics keyed to all ranges of the CRF

- Betting Range A: Up-as-you-win
- Betting Range B: Less aggressive up-as-you-win
- Betting Range C: Flat bet with regression on a loss
- Betting Range D & E: Flat betting to count reversal then using rules to increase your bet

Advanced Method 3: Betting tactics incorporating dealer breaks and winning rounds—summarized in Figure 16-1 on page (191)

Seventeen

HIGH-LOW-PLUS A WINNING STRATEGY FOR THE HANDHELD GAMES

DESCRIPTION OF THE STRATEGY

Traditional card-counting methods work best in single- and double-deck games. This is because, with only 52 or 104 cards in play, the game is more predictable. However, there are still biases in the single- and double-deck games that work in favor of either the player or the dealer. High-Low-Plus is based on the realities of today's game and delivers an edge to the astute player.

High-Low-Plus is a betting method based on the High-Low Count.

It will keep you in games in which you are winning; it gets you out of games in which you are losing. In winning games, High-Low-Plus maximizes your win and minimizes your loss. What more could you ask of a strategy?

First of all, find a single-deck game where three, four, or more rounds are dealt per deck before the shuffle or any double-deck game. This means that you should limit your games to those single-deck games with two or fewer other players. Ideally, including yourself, there should be no more than two other players in the game or no more than three hands dealt per round of play (not including the dealer's). For double-deck games, you could accept three other players in the game.

The basic concept involves determining your bet size, after the shuffle and at the start of the new game, by how you did in the last deck, whether you won or lost. Then you use the count to determine your bet size for your subsequent second and third hand of each deck.

In general, if you are winning, you increase your bet at the start of each game; if you are losing, keep it the same, reduce it, or depart the table.

RULES FOR DETERMINING HOW MUCH YOU BET AFTER THE SHUFFLE AT THE START OF EACH NEW GAME

The betting strategy below is detailed for a bet size off the top of the single-deck game; i.e., the first hand after the shuffle.

- Win two of three hands or three of four hands in prior deck: Increase bet by one unit (for first game upon table entry, bet one unit);

- Neither win nor lose in prior deck: bet same as last deck;

- Win one of three or fewer hands in last deck; i.e., any loss in last deck, reduce bet by 50 percent for first loss; reduce to one unit after second loss. Remember, here we are talking about a loss in the last deck, over three to four hands, not the loss of one hand.

The above rules are for the "plus" part of the High-Low-Plus Strategy. Next, I will discuss the rules for the "High-Low" portion of the strategy.

HOW TO USE THE HIGH-LOW COUNT TO MAKE THE BETTING DECISION AFTER THE FIRST HAND IN THE SINGLE-DECK GAME

As discussed previously, the High-Low Count involves assigning +1 to cards two–six, 0 to seven, eight, nine; and −1 to all tens, face cards, and aces. You keep a running count as each card is seen.

Here are the rules for using the count to decide how much to bet on your second and subsequent hand of each deck:

- Win last hand and plus count: Parley your bet; i.e., let everything ride;

- Win last hand and minus count: Bet same amount as last hand;

- Lose last hand and plus count: Bet same amount as last hand;

- Lose last hand and minus count: Reduce bet by 50 percent or bet just one unit.

OTHER RULES

Your buy-in amount is ten units. Your stop-loss is three–six units.

A conservative stop-win strategy is to lock up five units every time you win ten units and play until you lose the other five units. Example: Buy in for ten units. Win ten units. Lock up buy-in amount plus five-unit win, or fifteen units. Play with other five units until they are lost or until you win five more units. Each time your playing units equal ten, lock up five units and start over.

An aggressive stop-win strategy is, if you have won twenty units or more, continue playing until you give back no more than one third of your total win. Keep your total win in three equal-size stacks. Use one stack as your betting stack, and when that stack is gone, depart. If your betting stack grows larger than your other two stacks, be sure to keep the three stacks level by moving chips to the other two stacks. Every time you move chips in this manner, you are locking up money.

SINGLE- AND DOUBLE-DECK BETTING WITH THE COUNT

An alternative to High-Low-Plus and a more conservative strategy for the less aggressive player is to bet the running count in units in the single-deck game up to a maximum of four units. For example, if your running count is three at the end of round 1, bet three units for the next round; if two, bet two units, if zero or negative, bet one unit.

In the double-deck game, bet the running count minus one for the first deck, then bet the running count in units for rounds in the second deck of play. Keep your betting spread to four to one, the same as single-deck play.

I recommend a table stop-loss of ten units, and a trailing stop-loss of eight units; i.e., give back eight units from any high point win, leave the table.

There are some excellent strategies for single- and double-deck games described in my book *Casino Gambling* (Perigee Books, February 2000), which are compatible with the ideas presented in this chapter.

Eighteen

ON PLAYING BLACKJACK
FOR A LIVING

A FANTASY WORLD AND THE REAL WORLD OF
PROFESSIONAL BLACKJACK

There is a fantasy about playing professional blackjack and that is the idea of earning big bucks in a glamorous environment. It's the excitement of taking on the casinos and beating them at their own game. It's the security of having all the money you'll ever need. The fantasy even extends to the jet set. There's the dream of traveling the world, seeing exotic locations, meeting beautiful people, and paying all your expenses and then some by playing blackjack.

It's not that easy. Playing blackjack for a living is work the same as holding a job. And there are not that many gamblers who can hold up to the demands of the job.

There was Steve, for example. He was one of my most successful students in the days when I taught card counting. Single and with no debts or responsibilities, he decided to move to Las Vegas. Steve was under-bankrolled and he learned the hard way that the one and a half percent advantage of the card counter does not translate into instant riches. He also found out that the casinos don't like card counters; the pit bosses call them "undesirables" and list them in their black books in the same categories as cheats. Steve was a very disciplined player, but barely earned enough money to support himself. He quickly became fed up with the grind of casino play, returned East, and went back to work in the nine-to-five world.

Many of the would-be professionals I know make the move to Las Vegas. Mark was in this category, and he was under-bankrolled like many of the others. But he had one thing going for him—his wife worked. Mark played for small stakes and did all right in the beginning. But his winnings did not amount to much and he became impatient. Mark decided to take a shot and go for a big win with his small bankroll. Instead he took a hit and got blown out of the water.

Another player I know, an engineer, moved to Las Vegas and blew a bankroll. He lived on free hotdogs, available every afternoon at "Slots-a-Fun," for three weeks while he job hunted. (No, he'll never eat another hot dog as long as he lives!)

Those that fail usually do so because of a lack of knowledge of money management. They get the mistaken idea that a small bankroll can make them rich. And they have no notion of the discipline and mental attitudes that are required to become a successful pro.

The successful players have two attributes that are mandatory. One is their willingness to hold a part-time or even a full-time job while they build a large enough bankroll to make some big money. The other is their decision to learn how to win in other gambling games.

One player who made it learned how to play poker. He decided that winning money from other gamblers was easier than winning from the blackjack dealers. He continues to win at both the blackjack and poker tables.

Another became a horse handicapper. He spent mornings and some afternoons in the race book making $2 bets as he learned how to handicap. Evenings were spent at the blackjack tables. This person was also under-bankrolled, but he eked out a living for two years before giving up and returning East.

The Equalizer, mentioned in an earlier chapter (the person who built a bankroll from scratch), moved to Reno but held a full-time job for over two years while he built his blackjack bankroll. And he started with a zero bankroll! The Equalizer was successful for two reasons: (1) He learned that good discipline and mental preparation can overcome any barrier; and (2) he learned that record keeping is mandatory; table-by-table, and session summary records are used mainly for self-improvement and corrective action. And corrective action is what it's all about if your goal is to become a consistent, winning player and/or a semiprofessional or professional player.

The most successful "professional" blackjack player I know is a Christmas tree farmer from the state of Washington. He plays blackjack in the off-season—about half the time. And, when in Las Vegas, he doesn't play blackjack every day—about three days a week and only six hours on those three days. This person, we'll call him JT, knows his strengths and his weaknesses. He plays to his strengths and respects his weaknesses by following his schedule. This leaves him plenty of time to "smell the roses."

A 4-STAGE PLAN FOR BECOMING A PROFESSIONAL BLACKJACK PLAYER

Should you become a professional gambler? If you establish this goal, my advice is to proceed in stages. After you have learned the skills discussed in this book, you can establish a *4-Stage Plan* for turning professional.

Before discussing the plan, let me offer a new definition of a professional blackjack player. Playing professionally does not have to mean—in fact, should not mean—playing full-time for a living. My definition of a professional is a player who plays seriously, plays often, and uses blackjack as a means of generating profit to supplement his or her income. In a few cases it will mean playing full-time, but playing full-time only long enough to achieve one or two specific goals. The plan will explain this.

Before you begin the plan, be sure to read Barry Meadow's *Black-jack Autumn* discussed in Chapter 12 (and perhaps Stuart Perry's book as well: *Las Vegas Blackjack Diary*).

Stage 1

Stage 1 of the plan is to play part-time, acquire enough money to live on for at least six months, and build a reasonable-size bank-roll—at least $5000. You should also reduce your financial obligations to a minimum. You don't want the pressure of too many monthly payments clouding your judgment.

Stage 1 involves playing part-time for at least a six-month period, perhaps longer. This is a strategy that many players can easily adopt because of the plethora of gambling locations. Their overhead is low because they can schedule their sessions for a few hours, or a day or evening.

Stage 1 is your test period to determine whether or not you have the mettle to become a pro. If your blackjack profits are at an acceptable level for this period and you have accumulated the necessary funds, then you can proceed to Stage 2.

At the end of Stage 1, you should have six months of living expenses plus at least a $5000 bankroll.

Many would-be professionals will read this page and think to themselves, "Hey, I've got the money now; why wait? I don't need to play blackjack to establish my bankroll." Maybe you don't; but you should. It's as simple as this—if you can't win your bankroll at the tables, you probably should not turn pro.

Stage 2

Stage 2 of the plan involves traveling to a remote location for a temporary period of time. Go to Las Vegas or Atlantic City or Mississippi and play blackjack. Don't quit your job just yet. Take a leave of absence. Wait and see how you do. Now your objective is to make money plus pay for the increased overhead. Return home after the season and evaluate your situation. Is this what you want to do? Are you making enough money? Do you enjoy what you are doing? Do you want to continue in Stage 2 or proceed to Stage 3? Or perhaps even return to Stage 1, where you work part-time and play part-time?

Professional blackjack is work, the same as holding a job. Your learning should continue through the two stages described above. You should continue to perfect your techniques and expand and improve your skills. Stay abreast of what's happening in your new career field.

Stage 3

Stage 3 of the plan involves full-time play or serious part-time play and could involve a move to Las Vegas, Atlantic City, Mississippi, or another casino location. Most professionals choose Las Vegas for three reasons: (1) the variety of games offer more opportunities to make money; Atlantic City's games are standard six and eight decks with no rules variations; (2) other opportunities for making money abound; (3) the quality of life is much more pleasant; unlike Atlantic City, there are many pleasant diversions.

Atlantic City does have one major advantage not found elsewhere—the close proximity of the casinos to each other. If you don't find a game or table to your liking in one casino, it's just a short walk to the next one. Eleven casinos along the Boardwalk with a little over a mile separating them. The successful pros that I know who play Atlantic City don't move there. They come in for three or four day periods and then go back to their home base.

Most players who reach Stage 3 have established relationships with at least two other successful players. Many become part of or establish networks of successful players. These connections are not just for team or cooperative play; most players need the emotional support that comes from working with a group of peers.

Stage 4

Stage 4 of the plan is diversification. Choose a game you can beat other than blackjack. Diversification makes life much more interesting. Consider the following alternatives: roulette and craps. Each of these games offers much profit potential.

In craps, you gain an edge over the casino by learning how to set the dice and execute a controlled throw of the dice. Essentially, you create your advantage by reducing the chances of the losing seven occurring. To understand this concept of a controlled throw, all you need to know about craps is that, once you have established your winning number—four, five, six, eight, nine, or ten—you win if you throw this number before the seven shows. If you roll a seven, you lose. A seven has a higher likelihood of occurring than any other number. So what you must do in setting the dice is position them so that the sevens are out of the way, then throw them with a controlled throw to minimize the chances of the seven occurring. Easier said than done, but it is possible. See Section 6 for more information on how it's done and information on my home study course.

In roulette, you gain an edge by learning how to detect and exploit a dealer signature.

Many roulette dealers tend to repeat "near identical" conditions in many of their spins—not consciously, but due largely to repetition, or muscle memory. This repetition forms predictable patterns—or "signatures."

Many roulette dealers, no matter how skilled they are, or how hard they may try to "mix it up," will, to some degree, fall into this "repetition" pattern and form a clear signature.

Identifying the dealer signature enables the advantage player to predict the area of the wheel, or sector, into which the ball will fall.

Obviously not every time, but often enough to give you a measurable advantage over the casino.

For more information on my home study course for how to identify and exploit dealer signatures, consult Section 6.

Section Four

THE INTERNET—PITFALLS
AND POSSIBILITIES

Nineteen

TYPES OF BLACKJACK INFORMATION AVAILABLE ON THE INTERNET AND PROBLEMS IN ACCESSING IT

INTRODUCTION

More gambling information than you could ever hope to use is available to you on the Internet. For example, a search on "winning blackjack information" on the Altavista search engine produced a return of millions of web pages of information spread over hundreds of web sites. And to make matters more difficult, as we will discuss below, much of this information is worthless to the blackjack player looking to get an edge.

There is, indeed, a mountain of information out there in cyberspace and the question is how do you access it and sift out that which is usable to you? I researched this problem thoroughly for this book update, and will now share my findings with you.

In this chapter, after defining the problems associated with acquiring, evaluating and using blackjack information, I will show you how to sift through the huge amounts of information available. I will recommend search engines and directories that you can use to find this information on your own. I'll even suggest examples of keywords you can use to perform your search. In this way you will get the latest information available in the information categories to be described in this chapter. And you will derive the satisfaction of finding that information which satisfies your specific need.

The terms I use in this and the following two chapters—*Internet, World Wide Web (web, web site), online, cyberspace*—are defined as follows: *Internet* and *cyberspace* are synonymous, meaning that vast virtual world of information easily accessible on your computer via a modem and a telephone line; *online* means you are connected to and operating on the Internet; the *web* means web sites or locations you can visit in cyberspace, each having their own unique address.

Internet casinos operate on web sites. Blackjack Information is available on web sites.

You should also be familiar with the term "portal." A portal is a web site that is a "gateway" to other web sites, giving their Internet addresses and usually a hyperlink to them. A hyperlink can be thought of as a connector to transport you from one location to another in cyberspace. A hyperlink usually is displayed in a distinctive blue color; click on it with your mouse and away you go.

There are a great many gambling-related portals on the web, and we will describe and mention a few in this and the next two chapters.

The term "spam" as used in this chapter is an Internet-related term and means too much unwanted, unasked for sales messages coming to you via email or chat rooms or posted on newsgroups (defined below).

Categories of blackjack and gambling information sources available on the Internet include the following: (1) chat rooms, where you can talk with other players in real time; (2) newsgroups, where you can pose questions, get answers, and read other questions, answers, comments, gripes, complaints, etc. like a bulletin board; (3) list servers, which accept messages from gamblers and then distribute the messages to all subscribers to the list—either moderated or unmoderated; (4) web rings, which are web sites with a common subject linked to each other to make it easier to find and visit them; (5) web sites, which offer information and commercial products for sale; (6) e-zines (online e-mail newsletters or web sites that are up-dated periodically), which offer information about every conceivable gambling subject; and (7) directories and search engines.

It is fun to "surf the net" and visit new chat rooms, newsgroups, and web sites, but keep an open mind; better yet, keep a skeptical mind about the information you're examining. Be aware that you, and all gamblers surfing the net, are targets of Internet casinos; they want you as a customer and their tentacles reach into every corner of the web. The virtual world, i.e. the Net and the web, are where they reside and operate so, to stay competitive and make money, they have devised and implemented some very impressive and intense web-based marketing strategies. As a potential consumer of their service, you need to be aware of Internet casinos and their impact on blackjack information. We'll discuss them in detail in the next chapter.

Now let's get into detail about the seven sources of blackjack and gambling information.

CATEGORY 1: CHAT ROOMS

Some gamblers enjoy participating in chat rooms, meeting other players, and exchanging dialog in real time. Friendships can develop and information can be exchanged.

There are scores of blackjack and gambling-related chat rooms available on the Internet. Many are associated with online casinos. Online casinos offer chat rooms because they want gamblers to feel comfortable on their sites. If you enjoy chatting it up and talking to other gamblers, you are more likely to play at the casino making the chat room available.

Other chat rooms are associated with authors of blackjack books, many of whom charge you for the privilege of entering their room. Card-counting discussions dominate most of these types of chat rooms.

Keep in mind that, unless they are selling something, most participants in chat rooms remain anonymous. This is one of the main benefits of the Internet, anyone can say anything they want, express any opinion, comment on any subject, even act like an expert giving "expert opinions," with no fear of any recriminations.

In addition to those gamblers who are legitimately searching for gambling information and gambling dialogs, and are consciously attempting to provide answers and information, I have observed the following three trends regarding who participates in chat rooms and other forms of internet communication discussed below:

(1) Gamblers with little or no experience, maybe just enough experience to be dangerous, who enjoy playing the expert and spending many hours surfing the net and responding/communicating/posting messages in chat rooms and newsgroups;

(2) Web site operators and system sellers who invite you to visit their web site to read whatever selling message they have to deliver, many of whom tout the Internet casinos;

(3) Internet casino operators, webmasters, and shills, who tout their casino(s), its advantages, like signing bonuses, and strongly urge you to visit their web sites.

CATEGORY 2: NEWSGROUPS

Blackjack newsgroups are different from chat rooms in that messages are posted on an electronic bulletin board, which can then be responded to or not depending on the inclination of the visitor. You must go to the newsgroup to read and post messages. You will see messages posted by experienced gamblers, beginners, kooks who have their own ax to grind, experts, and Internet casino operators. You can pose questions for others to respond to, you can respond to others' questions, and you can comment on any aspect of gambling you wish. All messages are posted on the newsgroups' bulletin boards for all to see and read as they choose. Some newsgroups are moderated, which means that a moderator looks at each message before it is posted to determine whether or not it meets the newsgroup's criteria as being fit to post.

The most popular of the blackjack newsgroups are rec.gambling.blackjack and rec.gambling.blackjack.moderated, each of which has scores of messages posted every day.

For rec.gambling.blackjack, messages break down along the following lines:

- messages from online casinos that offer answers to questions posed, but give you a link to or the address of their online casino and a reason to visit it;

- messages from webmasters promoting their web sites as sources of blackjack information and inviting you to visit by clicking on a hyperlink embedded in their post; at many such sites you will find enticements to visit the online casinos with which the Webmaster is associated;

- out and out spam promoting links to online casinos or other money-making schemes;

- legitimate questions from blackjack players looking for answers; e.g. where can I find one- or two-deck games in Las Vegas?;

- trip reports from gamblers, some complete with pictures, containing details of their winning trips and how they did it, and also many containing advice (usually outdated) on good deals on where to eat, stay, travel, etc.;

- invitations from systems sellers to visit their site, at which you will find descriptions of books and systems for sale;

- news reports on who's doing what in the world of gambling and casinos; i.e. who's selling which property, who's moving up, who died, which casino is up for sale, or sold, etc.;

- debates about some aspect of gambling that can carry on for hours or even days or weeks; usually these debates will start with the participants on friendly terms with each side presenting its opinions in a logical manner, but if the subject being debated is controversial, it may quickly break down with participants on each side hurling insults at each other. A total of fifty-seven messages comprised one recent debate with the ending message from a neutral person being: *Many of us are (too) forthcoming on these NGs, and there is a nonnegligible risk that people who are not well-informed will be persuaded by those with the facade of expertise in the area of games of chance.* Very good advice, indeed.

I estimate that more than 50 percent of the messages posted to rec.gambling.blackjack are posted by online casinos and their representatives, by system sellers, and by hucksters promoting get-rich-quick schemes.

The other notable blackjack newsgroup is rec.gambling.blackjack. moderated. Since this one is moderated, i.e. looked at by a person with the authority to either post the message or not, spam usually doesn't get posted.

But this group is dominated by traditional blackjack players, authors, and webmasters who repudiate any blackjack method, strategy or idea that is outside the bounds of their traditional card-counting theories.

These days I generally make it a point to stay away from the gambling-related newsgroups. I find them to be very time-consuming and mostly a forum for hotheads who stubbornly spew uninformed opinions. Granted, bits of useful information can be found from time to time. But, once I've weeded out the spam and the inane debate threads, I find that it's simply not worth the time. That's me, though. If you're the type who thrives on debate and have the time, these newsgroups can provide a never-ending supply of arguments and discussions to join.

CATEGORY 3: LIST SERVERS

Gambling list servers operate a little differently—any message posted is automatically sent to the email address of all participants. Depending on the activity in the list you belong to, you may get several messages a day. Some lists give the participant the ability to restrict the timing and length of messages delivered. You have to decide on your level of involvement. I am aware of a few list servers that are used by blackjack players for networking purposes. In some, depending on who belongs, you may find yourself receiving spam email messages sent through the list from a participant trying to make a buck or two.

If you are an active blackjack player with many blackjack-playing friends, consider setting up your own network on a list server. Many web sites offer list server software at no cost. And the software is relatively easy to set up.

One such web site is eGroups. Email groups allow for easy group communication and interaction through the ease and convenience of email. For details visit: http://www.groupsyahoo.com

CATEGORY 4: WEB RINGS

Web rings are another source of gambling information. A web ring consists of member sites banding together to form their own sites into linked circles. This allows more visitors to reach them quickly and easily. The quickest way to find a blackjack or gambling ring is to visit web rings online directory at: http://www.dir.webring.yahoo.com/vw.

Here you can select a category or search across the Internet for rings of interest. if you can't find a ring that suits your interest, you are free to start your own.

But here's the catch: Internet casinos and web sites promoting Internet casinos dominate the blackjack and gambling-oriented web rings. Is there a web ring that will serve you up usable, unbiased information that can impact your game? Hopefully, there will be by the time you are reading this book.

CATEGORY 5: WEB SITES AND PORTALS

There are literally hundreds of gambling-oriented and blackjack web sites, most of which are trying with all kinds of gimmicks and fancy/flashing images to grab your attention.

Many of these web sites are sales oriented, but some offer free information as well. A few are run as hobbies and genuinely attempt to provide useful information to gamblers surfing the Net.

Many web sites offering casino gambling information have Internet casino affiliations, that is they take a cut of each gamblers' losses or a percentage of initial and subsequent deposits of gamblers they recommend or direct to their client casinos. Although we have nothing against this, be careful of a potential conflict of interest, and regard it as a normal business decision. Make sure the web site has your interests at heart and not the casino's.

On the other hand, some Internet casinos recruit noted gambling authors to write articles and answer players' questions about the games. Many gambling-oriented sites on the web are sponsored and paid for by Internet casinos. But don't let the flashing lights and colorful and fancy sites seduce you; they're just another strategy to lure you into one of the casinos promoted on the site.

Casino.com

However, there is one portal that's worth a visit if you are a traditional player and are interested in learning how to count cards: casino.com. Casino.com, sponsored by Boss Media, a portal for twenty-eight online casinos (probably more by the time you read this), does a good job of delivering basic player-oriented gambling information. If you are interested in blackjack, craps, roulette, poker, and slots, you'll find gambling authors here who will answer your basic questions. Their objective, of course, is to educate you and keep you coming back for more so that, eventually, you'll take a shot at one of their online casinos.

Is it possible to ferret out any bonafide web sites that offer blackjack information unfettered by any casino influence? I'll answer this question in the concluding remarks at the end of this chapter.

CATEGORY 6: E-ZINES AND NEWSLETTERS

There are a wide ranging number of gambling newsletters and e-zines (refers to an online newsletter or web site dispensing information) available to the interested gambler. In fact, I subscribed to over twenty in the process of researching this book.

Most gambling web sites you visit will attempt to obtain your e-mail address in return for sending you an email newsletter. I've mentioned before what their purpose is — mainly to send you online casino advertisements. Since it's fairly simple to have your name removed from these lists, I suggest sampling a few. To avoid the possibility of receiving unsolicited e-mail (spam), I suggest setting up a free e-mail account at yahoo.com.

When you visit casino.com, you can subscribe to three newsletters: *The Spin, Casino Wire,* and *Ask the Pro,* the latter dispensing gambling advice. *The Spin* is the house organ delivering updates on the Boss Media Casinos and promoting the gambling authors' sites, while *Casino Wire* keeps you updated on the casino industry in general.

CATEGORY 7: INTERNET DIRECTORIES AND SEARCH ENGINES

The World Wide Web contains well over a billion pages of material, and this huge mountain of information is growing by leaps and bounds every day. To find what you are looking for on the World Wide Web, it is necessary to use a search vehicle—either a search engine or a directory.

A search engine, using your keywords, searches a portion of the entire Internet and then displays its results in a listing that may contain several thousand pages and scores of web sites. Search engines use powerful software, called "spiders," which continuously search the Net for new or changed web sites and then automatically index them into a voluminous database. Directories differ in that they are indexed by human beings, not software. A search engine will ask for keywords while a directory gives you the option of searching a hierarchy of information categories. An example of a search engine is altavista (altavista.com). An example of a directory is yahoo (yahoo.com).

Even with these sophisticated software aids, finding exactly what you want can be tricky because of the tremendous volume of information and the Internet casinos and their affiliated web sites that permeate the search engines' data bases. It is extremely difficult, if not impossible, for a search engine or directory to return information on any search keywords you can devise for blackjack or gambling without it being tainted directly or indirectly by the Internet casinos.

THE EMERGING SOLUTION

Is there any independent web site or portal that evaluates and ranks gambling-oriented web sites? Unfortunately, at the time of this writing, only a few exist, which I'll cover in the next chapter. Some web sites purport to do this now, but either don't go far enough or use their listing of gambling-oriented web sites as a sales tool to get you to bite and leave your email address.

Some web sites participate in affiliate programs as a means of earning income for the work they put into their sites. Some are able to avoid affiliate programs because they have strong secured advertising contracts, but in actual fact these are more often the sites to be wary of because in many cases they are actually fronts for a casino, or recommend only their key advertisers.

There are a number of other ways to distinguish fair reviews from "red herrings," or fronts, for the casinos:

- Web site does not hide the fact that it benefits from affiliate programs;

- Web site does not accept advertising or participate in affiliate programs from low-quality casinos;

- Web site typically goes out of its way to respond to gamblers' needs in emails or forums;

- Web site is not covered in banner ads.

In order for a web site to spend the time to independently review casinos or gambling sites, it has to be financially secure enough to invest the time and money promoting gambling or be able to make income from the effort and time it puts in.

There is no distinguishing between the two save for affiliate programs and ads. One has to be careful accepting advice from anyone on any issue—you must take the time to read through and judge for yourself.

Very often, good web sites will have exchanges or links to each other, not free-for-all listings, or extensive directories. Though recommendations based on their own personal play and reports from players they trust, some web sites deliver fairly accurate information. In such cases all the prospective gambler needs to do is establish that they are not owned by the same company, and they meet the criteria listed above. Once you find a good web site or two, you will usually be able to find more that are linked in some way.

In the meantime, I suggest having some fun in your own quest to find information that may be useful to you. Visit the Looksmart.com and the open directory (dmoz.org) and poke around in their gambling segments and see what you can find. Go to the Altavista.com search engine and try a few searches. The key words you can use are limited only by your imagination. Try these to start: winning gambling systems, winning blackjack systems, blackjack advantage systems, blackjack web sites and blackjack e-zines. Count the Internet casinos that are listed in the first twenty or thirty entries and see how many show up.

Above all, follow the advice in this chapter; be skeptical until the web site proves it has your best interests at heart. If you find a web site that you believe to be independent and free of casino influence, contact me and I will check it out for you.

By the time you read this book, a clearinghouse for such web sites may be available. For current information, use the information request form in the back of this book.

Twenty

THE INTERNET CASINOS—
PITFALLS AND POSSIBILITIES

In the prior chapter, I discussed the influence of the Internet casinos on the Internet and, more particularly, on blackjack information available from the Internet.

In this chapter I will go into much more detail about this new industry by discussing the issues surrounding Internet casinos and by showing you how to select one at which you can play with confidence. This will lay the foundation for the next chapter, which will describe winning methods for gaining an advantage in online blackjack games.

Let's get started.

BACKGROUND

To understand the dominance of Internet casinos on blackjack information, it is first necessary to examine this new industry and discuss the issues related to it.

Internet casinos offer a gambling experience unlike that offered by real casinos in that the games are delivered right to your computer screen in the comfort of your home or office, any time of the day or night. There are about eight hundred Internet casinos in operation as this book is being written; by the time you are reading it, probably one thousand or more will be in existence. Over three million gamblers visited an Internet casino in 1999. It is estimated that this number will increase to over 16 million by 2002 (Boss Media Company). Their losses are estimated to soar from $1.2 billion to $3 billion (Bear, Sterns & Co.).

No Internet casino is actually located in the U.S. Many are located in the Caribbean on island nations such as Antigua and the Dominican Republic, who welcome them because of the license fees they generate. Others are located in Canada, Australia, and South Africa. The casinos in these locations are not like the casinos that we walk into expecting to find blackjack tables with a dealer dealing cards out of a shoe. An Internet casino exists as powerful software residing on a large-scale computer programmed to make its games available through web sites that anyone can tap into on the Internet. You access this software and play the games either by downloading the appropriate portion of it to your hard drive or through your browser.

Internet casinos permeate all aspects of gambling information available on the World Wide Web. The reasons are: size of this new industry, its rapid rate of growth, and the extreme competitive nature of the Internet casinos. Compare the numbers to get an idea — about eight hundred Internet casinos to about four hundred land-based casinos in all of the U.S. And these eight hundred Internet casinos are all offering compelling messages to casino gamblers to solicit their business, competing with each other to take the gamblers' money, and fighting for survival in the virtual world of cyberspace.

In describing the problems Internet casinos are causing gamblers who are looking for information, it is important to understand their two major advantages over land-based casinos: (1) their cost of doing business (overhead) is much less in that they require no physical property and their operations are mostly computer-based, not people-based; (2) their marketing costs are much less because of the special nature of World Wide Web directories and search engines.

Our main purpose in assessing this new gambling industry is to warn you about the pitfalls of Internet casinos so that, if you decide to gamble in cyberspace, you will be armed with sufficient information to make an intelligent choice of which casino to play. Let's start by discussing the issues.

THE ISSUES SURROUNDING INTERNET CASINOS

Issue 1: Legality

Legality is a major issue and there are currently bills before the U.S. Congress to outlaw Internet casinos as this book goes to press. Some states, such as Missouri and South Dakota, have passed laws prohibiting Internet casinos from offering their games of chance within state boundaries. But even if the federal law passes (named the Kyl Bill after the Congressman sponsoring it), it will be extremely difficult, if not impossible, to police its provisions and stop you or I from tapping into these casinos from the privacy of our homes. I must, however, caution you that if you live in any state that proscribes gambling on the Internet, I urge you not to break the law.

There is much controversy and differences of opinion on the legality issue, but based on my research, I believe that Internet casinos are here to stay regardless of laws passed by the states or federal government. They have found their niche in the gambling industry, they are making money, and they are riding a wave of gambling growth that began in 1987 when the federal government made it legal for Indian nations to open casinos. A few of these Internet casinos are even publicly held companies listed on the NASDAQ; e.g. Boss Media, an Internet portal for a number of online casinos and that owns the nifty www.casino.com domain name.

With all of these facts taken into account, I have reached the conclusion that these casinos are viable, and we need to assess them for play as we would any land-based casino.

Issue 2: Honesty and Fairness

The honesty issue concerns whether or not you can get your money back promptly any time you request it from one of these outfits. From my initial study of the Internet casino industry, I have reached the conclusion that most casinos are honest. The key word here is "most." If you decide to risk money, you need to know about the casino at which you are considering play. If you send money to them via a credit card, can you get at your initial stake and any accrued winnings whenever you wish and expect a prompt return of the money requested? To get an answer to this question you need to check the ratings of the casino you intend to visit. I'll show you how to do that later in this chapter.

The main issue, however, in assessing Internet casinos is fairness. How do you know the games are fair? Most any casino you visit will explain its random number generator that drives the games. They will tell you that any number has the same chance of occurring as any other number; therefore any hand of blackjack, any number thrown at craps, or any spin result at roulette is perfectly random, they say. They go on to say that if there is a bias, it can work to the benefit of the players as well as the house. If a player bias occurs, word would get around the Internet very quickly, players would exploit it, and quickly break the casino.

Some Internet casinos have their software audited by one of the big six accounting firms to guarantee that the software is working fairly. I found one casino who posts its payout numbers for all the games on a monthly basis. These numbers compare favorably with industry standards. I expect posting the payout numbers will be a trend picked up by other casinos because of competitive reasons.

Based on my research, I believe it is reasonable to make the assumption that most cyberspace casinos are fair. The sheer size of this growing industry also contributes to exposing the bad apples, by players and by the casinos' competition. Still, the nagging question remains—do they cheat?

How do we really know whether or not an Internet casino isn't cheating us? I mean, couldn't they easily design their software to slip a few extra fives into a blackjack game (thus giving the dealer a much higher advantage) for a millisecond or two every once in a while? Or throw an extra seven at the craps table when the player(s) are loaded up on their bets? Then easily skim this money into a secret bank account, all the while bypassing the log files that their accounting firm audits? This is certainly within the state of the art.

From the opposing point of view, why cheat when you have the odds working for you? And a low overhead to boot? The idea is to develop a good reputation, take care of your customers, give them good signing bonuses, develop an affiliate program to drive new customers to your casino, and you will make money. Many of the big casino portals do just that. Some, like Boss Media, actually go a step further. Boss Media purchases "genuine random numbers." Not relying on the random numbers ("pseudo-random numbers") that most casino software generates, they purchase random numbers based on radioactive decay. In this way, the firm that delivers this service claims, it is not possible for either side—casino or player— to doctor the random numbers or detect any inherent pattern. This topic will be taken up further in the next chapter when we discuss winning strategies.

If you are gambling online or decide to visit an Internet casino, you should proceed with caution and collect as much information as possible about the casino you intend to visit. I'll have more to say about choosing a casino later in this chapter.

INTERNET CASINO MARKETING STRATEGIES

With over eight hundred casinos in operation, the industry is extremely competitive. A marketing strategy that produces a steady stream of new customers is crucial to each casino's success.

One strategy you should be aware of is web sites that rate and rank Internet casinos. Many web sites claim to evaluate and rate listed casinos, and this may very well be true. But the problem is that some web sites may be fronts for certain casinos with the angle that they, and only they, know who the honest operators are; they have rated and ranked these casinos and they will introduce you to them and get you a nice signing bonus to stake you to your first play. Click here and away you go to their recommended casino with the web site's ID following you through cyberspace to insure that they get a piece of your action (a commission on player deposits, some as high as 25 percent).

Before attempting to get your quick click to one of their affiliated casinos, however, many web sites attempt to induce you to enter your email address with the promise of sending you a periodic gambling e-zine with all kinds of useful information. While some of these e-zines are an honest attempt to publish useful information for the casino gambler, in many cases they use your address to send you email messages about their client casinos, touting their many advantages like signing bonuses, prizes, good games, easily downloadable software, and other benefits.

The Internet casino marketing gambit that is of major interest to us as players is the signing bonus offered by most Internet casinos, usually at least 20 percent on your initial deposit, and, in some cases, during special promotions, 20 percent or more on subsequent deposits. This up-front signing bonus is like getting free money, and, if properly invested using a winning strategy, is like money in the bank for the astute Internet blackjack player. Specific advantage strategies will be described in the next chapter.

CHOOSING AN INTERNET CASINO

Before you play at any Internet casino, here are some questions you should ask:

- Is the casino licensed by their host country?

- Do they have a reputation for making prompt payouts?

- Is their software audited by an independent accounting firm?

- Do they use software acquired from one of the big gaming software firms? Or did they develop their game software in-house?

- Do they post their payouts for each game on a monthly basis?

- Have they been in business long enough to establish a bettor-friendly track record?

- Is their record free of customer complaints?

- Do they use third-party payment systems to take the risk out of withdrawing money from your account?

- Do they have an easily accessible, friendly, and helpful customer service department?

- Do they use the traditional random number generator or do they acquire true random numbers based on radioactive decay?

Answers to many of these questions can be obtained by contacting the casinos' customer service departments or talking to the casino personnel, including the casino manager.

But you really need to check them out on your own by examining rankings and ratings of the casinos you are interested in visiting. Start your analysis at the web sites described next.

Rankings, Ratings, and Evaluations of Internet Casinos

With close to eight hundred Internet casinos to choose from, the first step in the process is to find a reputable web site you can trust that checks out and ranks Internet casinos based on some or all of the criteria listed above. As noted in the previous chapter, there are currently few if any web sites that offer this service. We expect this situation to change, however, as the need for such a service increases dramatically because of the large number of new gamblers entering cyberspace. Because of the dynamic nature of the Internet, I will list and recommend only a few web sites here—those that I have personally checked out and believe will be around for a long duration. Others I leave out because I am uncertain about their viability or their evaluation criteria. Contact me using the contact information in the back of this book, and I'll send you my list of current recommended web sites.

The best way for you to start is to go to the Internet Gaming Commission, an independent outfit not taking advertising from any casino. They maintain a web site listing licensed and unlicensed Internet casinos. Their staff includes accountants, system engineers, and experienced gamblers. On their site you will find links to the casinos they monitor and evaluate where you can read of the experiences other gamblers have had with various Internet casinos. You can visit their site at www.internetcommission.com.

This outfit is leading the way for Internet casinos to adopt self-regulatory policies and has plans for becoming the dominant web site to support online gamblers who want impartial data about the casinos they visit.

You can use this site to select a casino for further evaluation or to evaluate a casino at which you are considering play.

Here are two web sites which you can check for casino recommendations featuring ratings based on web site evaluations and player reports: www.got2bet.com and www.casinomeister.com. They are both affiliated with Internet casinos, but they do seem to have the Internet gamblers' best interests as their first priority, and they are honest about their casino affiliations showing them right up front.

To give you an idea of the kind of evaluation report that responds to and answers many of the above questions, I have included a sample evaluation report that follows, prepared by an Internet friend who plays extensively and does thorough evaluations. I have left the name of the casino in the report so you can check it out at the Internet Commission and get a current report. Be sure to do that before you play or just for practice to get some experience.

Casino-on-net Evaluation Report (www.casino-on-net.com)

This online casino has been around over four years now and has well established itself in the online casino community. At any given time, you'll find many high rollers playing. After spending five days playing at their tables at various times of the day, here is the good, the bad, and the ugly, though not necessarily in that order.

WEBSITE
You enter the site with downloadable software. A simple and straightforward gaming site. No distracting glitziness or silliness to get in the way of business. All subcategories are easy to navigate.

PLAY
Casino-on-net offers a 20 percent one-time compensation of your initial deposit upon opening a new account with them. At the time I signed in, they even had a special one-day-only additional 10 percent. Once you're on their mailing list, you'll find Casino-on-net has a multitude of special offers, including better than average buy-in bonuses for current players. The only requirement is you must play an amount equal to the bonus before withdrawal. Fair enough since many casinos require you to play your entire buy-in before allowing you to cash out. You are given three choices of tables to

play at. You can play at a private table, you can open your own table and play with predetermined players such as your pals, or you can play at a public table and powwow with other players. I've talked to many personable and happy players here. Players are allowed to bet anywhere from $1 and up, no limits. This $1 minimum bet is a rarity. You can also check your recent playing history anytime. This is free of charge.

ODDS

Though I played at a few of the games offered, I decided to do a complete evaluation of the blackjack tables including private and public tables. Having played over six hundred hands for this evaluation, my own spreadsheets determined a better than 52 percent loss/win ratio. This is better than Vegas odds, though it's a small sample, but still reassuring. The total of blackjack wins were also slightly better than average, indicating the casino probably hasn't removed tens and aces from the random card programming, which would give the house an unfair edge. Even though few casinos do this, it's always good to be aware of the possibility; blackjack play is tough enough without giving the house an unfair added edge.

SUPPORT

There is no toll-free number to call their support staff as of this writing. According to the support manager at Casino-on-net, they don't feel the need for the added expense. Any questions must be answered via email. My questions (and I asked a lot of questions) were answered in a timely and knowledgeable manner, though that wasn't the case several months ago when I first dabbled on this casino. It was easy to tell they've made strides for better and faster customer service. Casino-on-net's support staff seems to be able to handle any question you throw at them, again, better than the average casino that shares toll-free numbers with many other casinos in the same group.

CASHING OUT

Easy to do with only a small peeve. Casino-on-net doesn't cash out your money immediately. Instead, they put it into a hold status for five business days. Their reasoning for this is to make your funds easier to access in case you change your mind. Mind you, I haven't found many sites that are any faster. Any monies up to and including the amount withdrawn from your credit card will be credited back to that card. Additional funds can be sent to you either via cashier's check or a direct wire transfer to your bank, it's your choice. There is no charge for this service. That's a refreshing thought, eh?

THE BOTTOM LINE

You won't get hurt at Casino-on-net. This casino was one of the first and they intend to be around a long time. This site is as honest as they come with good odds. By some of the unimaginably huge wagering I saw, many big-time gamblers must find the odds highly acceptable here. I'll be making trips back.

Author's Note: The above evaluation report is printed as information only and is not to be construed as an endorsement or recommendation of any kind.

OFFLINE GAMBLING MAGAZINES

Many slick, gambling-oriented magazines contain articles on Internet casinos. More will come into existence as the online-casino industry continues to grow and spend money on advertising. Most, if not all, of these magazines feature the advertisements of many Internet casinos. In fact, one could say the Internet casino ads dominate their pages. Many articles within their pages evaluate, extol the features of, rate, and rank the same Internet casinos that advertise within their pages. It is possible that a magazine could be a front for a ring of Internet casinos.

Can you trust this kind of information? Would you play at an

Internet casino who advertised in the pages of such a magazine and was evaluated and recommended within those same pages? I would urge caution.

You can find many of these magazines by going to altavista.com and entering keywords "casino magazines." The keyword "casino" suggest their true orientation—to promote the online casinos.

CHOOSING AN INTERNET CASINO BASED ON ITS SOFTWARE PACKAGE AND PUBLIC ACCEPTANCE

To operate in cyberspace, an Internet casino must have software—the computer programs that are displayed on your computer screen, the software they supply for you to play the games when you enter their URL and click the Go button.

The casino can acquire this software in one of two ways: (1) by developing it themselves or (2) by acquiring it from a reputable third-party software firm.

When you select a casino for play, I recommend choosing one that acquired its software, under license, from a reputable third-party software vendor. This gives one more confidence in the honesty and integrity of the casino. An in-house staff, under local management control, might be tempted to up the odds just a little bit by deleting a ten-value card here and there from their blackjack game. I'm not suggesting that a casino would do this, but why not go with the casino at which this question should never even arise?

The next question is the choice of software package. Should you consider this when evaluating an online casino for play? By all means yes. The extreme growth of the online casino industry is contributing to the growth of gaming software industry; just as more and more online casinos are being formed, so more and more gaming software firms are getting into this lucrative business.

It is beyond the scope of this book to teach you how to evaluate, rate, rank, and choose which gaming software package to opt for;

this function will become part of your search for reputable web sites that rate and rank the casinos.

But I will get you started by describing here what I believe is software outfit that can be your starting point for online casino play—Boss Media.

There are other Internet casino outfits out there who may be just as good, if not better, than Boss Media. If and when you evaluate them, use the points I make below as the basis for comparison.

My purpose in presenting these reasons for choosing Boss Media is to get you off to the right start should you decide to venture into cyberspace to play blackjack.

Here are the main features for Boss Media (www.bossmedia.com):

- Boss Media was formed in 1997. They are a public company listed on the Swedish Stock Exchange's O-list in June 1999 under the symbol (BOSS). You can get their financial information by going to www.streetdice.com.

- They have licensed 36 casinos as this book is written (26 up and running), and they are growing fast with online casino acceptance and player acceptance of their downloadable software. It is interesting that one of these online casinos is owned by the Swedish government: Svenska Spel's Casino Cosmopol.

- Their license fee is more expensive than most other firms, which means to us, as blackjack players, their software is probably more comprehensive, easier to use, and faster than other software packages. Their higher fee may also explain their extremely comprehensive background check on their licensees.

- They seem to offer a more complete turnkey business model to their licensees going beyond the delivery of software and into management and personnel support in the administrative, financial, and customer support areas. Other outfits offer these functions as an option to their licensees, but Boss Media builds them in to each licensee's contract. A major reason is to maintain and nurture the very favorable reputation they have developed in the online gambling field.

- They use PriceWaterhouseCoopers to audit their gross payouts and insure that these conform to the expected mathematical odds.

- They use a third party, Webdollar, to handle all deposits and withdrawals, which means that it is easy and there are no hassles when you decide to withdraw your money (although Webdollar is a wholly owned subsidiary of Boss Media).

- They use genuine random numbers for every hand dealt at blackjack and other casino games that they offer.

- They are a player-oriented Internet gaming firm offering access to gambling authors at their casino portal — www.casino.com.

Now let's get to the bottom line — how do you beat these guys? On to the next chapter.

Twenty-one

HOW TO GET AN EDGE AT INTERNET CASINO BLACKJACK GAMES

The methods in this chapter assume you are getting a fair game as defined in the last chapter, that you are getting at least a 20 percent signing bonus, and that you are using Basic Strategy to play the hands.

What that 20 percent signing bonus means is that you have an actual edge over the casino with the bankroll representing your deposit plus your signing bonus. Let's say you are playing blackjack with perfect Basic Strategy, which is about a half percent casino edge. Factoring in the signing bonus of 20 percent, you are playing with an edge of 19.5 percent with this initial bankroll. Keep in mind that this edge only applies to the initial bankroll. You will learn in Method 2 in this chapter how and when to "reacquire" this advantage by opening up accounts periodically at new casinos.

METHOD 1: PLAYING AGAINST THE RANDOM-NUMBER-GENERATED BLACKJACK GAME

All Internet casinos use random number generators (RNG) to determine the cards dealt, the number thrown with a pair of dice, the spin result at roulette, or the outcome of a video poker game or a pull on the slot machine.

Random Number Generators

Before I discuss the strategy, a little background on RNGs is necessary.

According to some authorities, numbers calculated by a computer through a deterministic process cannot, by definition, be random. The question boils down to prediction. Given knowledge of the computer algorithm, one could predict the sequence of these numbers and thus gain a huge edge over the online casino.

In dealing, then, with online casinos, we must recognize two types of random numbers: pseudo random numbers and genuine random numbers. This recognition presents us with two choices in gaining the edge: (1) Given a choice, we should prefer to play at a casino using genuine random numbers because predictable sequences can be used both ways—by the casino to cheat (although I am not implying any casinos do this, it is possible) and by players to gain an edge with accurate prediction information (assuming the players could figure out the algorithm and thus the sequence of events); (2) even though we haven't figured out the algorithm, pseudo random numbers may present us with blackjack game patterns that may be predictable.

For more information on pseudo versus genuine random numbers, you may wish to visit a web site that generates genuine random numbers through a process involving radioactive decay: http://www.fourmilab.ch/hotbits.

I realize that there is some ambiguity in the above two choices, but this is the current state of the art and it brings us to the first idea for gaining an edge.

Assuming these games are dealt with no fixed number of decks, back-and-forth or choppy games could occur if Basic Strategy is used to play the hands. The strong dealer-biased games that result from like-card clumping should not be evident. Based on these assumptions, Step 1 is to play Basic Strategy with a 3-level negative betting progression in the "Play Free" mode that most Internet casinos offer. If you find yourself in a choppy game; i.e., back-and-forth winning between you and the dealer, try a minor negative progression like one-two-four. Bet one unit; if you lose, bet two units; lose again, bet four units. Lose three in a row, end the session or start over reverting to a table minimum flat bet. Any win in the three hands results in a one-unit profit; a win starts the progression over. If the game continues choppy, increase your spread to one-three-seven.

Play this simple method in the free play mode with no money at risk. Get a feel for the patterns in the casino's RNG. Are there patterns? Is the game choppy? How long does the chop last before you lose seven or eleven units? Did your winning prior to the loss of a progression cover the loss? Is a winning choppy pattern evident over several successive days of play? If you find recurring choppy periods, try a hit-and-run strategy grabbing five units or six units, then moving on to another casino and coming back to this one at a later time.

You could open accounts at several casinos and play the up-as-you-lose three-level progression at those where you find the choppy patterns. If nothing else, you're having fun in the play-free mode with no money at risk, and it's quite possible that you will find a game that would warrant risking real money, in which case you would make a deposit at that casino.

Important: In the beginning, I recommend playing only at Boss Media casinos for reasons given in the last chapter, especially the fact that they all offer games based on genuine random numbers. These games, perhaps, are more suited for this and other methods to be described below. Later, as you gain experience, you may wish to play at casinos offering games based on pseudo random numbers.

When playing at casinos using pseudo random numbers, it is important that, when converting from Free Play to playing with real money, you confirm that the real money game is similar to the free play game. That is, you are looking for the same choppy back-and-forth game.

I have heard reports from some online gamblers that once they put real money into action, the game changes from choppy to a losing trend. So, you need to set a stop-loss for each casino at which you open an account—between 20 percent and 50 percent of your deposit—depending on the risk you are prepared to take. I am not suggesting that your losing happens because of casino cheating, but why take the risk? A casino stop-loss is good money management practice in any event.

METHOD 2: EXPLOITING THE INTERNET CASINOS' CASH BONUSES

The fact that hundreds of Internet casinos are all competing with each other for customers and offering cash bonuses to get them and keep them offers gamblers a unique opportunity to turn the tables and gain the advantage.

Because of this intense competition, many Internet casinos offer a 20 percent signing bonus when you open an account. Some casinos will credit you with a 20 percent signing bonus on subsequent deposits. Sometimes, during holidays and other special dates, they will raise this bonus to as much as 50 percent of your deposit. Their usual policy on this money is that you must generate betting action equal to or greater than your entire deposit plus signing bonus before you can withdraw the money.

These signing bonuses are the equivalent of comps in the real-world casinos, but there is one huge difference—you get them up front, before you make that first bet. Can you imagine walking into a real-world casino, sitting down at a blackjack table, buying in for $100 and being given $120 worth of chips? "What's this for?" you ask. "It's yours," says the dealer. "All we ask is that you give us at least $120 worth of action before leaving the table." Would you accept the extra $20 under these conditions? Of course you would!

The tactic, then, when playing blackjack at the Internet casinos is to use a conservative betting strategy to generate betting action equal to or greater than your deposit plus signing bonus and then withdraw the money. Assuming that you break even or even lose a little, the signing bonus gives you the edge. After the withdrawal, repeat the tactic at another casino.

You could use the betting tactic from Method 1 above to generate your action and then play as long as your game is predictable; i.e., as long as you are getting a choppy back-and-forth game in which you are able to grind out a few units per session, stay with this casino. When your game turns sour, or is no longer predictable, close your account, withdraw your money, and play at another casino. Your objective is to close your account with a win and the upfront bonus gives you the cushion to do just that. This assumes that your betting action is equal to or greater than your original deposit plus signing bonus, which is the casinos' requirement before they will refund the signing bonus along with your deposit.

If Method 1 is working and you have ground out units in a choppy game, which are equal to or greater than your deposit plus your signing bonus, set a trailing stop-loss that, if triggered, would signal the withdrawal and account closing. I recommend fourteen units for the stop-loss amount. This is the loss of two of the one-two-four progressions. If you lose both right up front, before winning any money or giving the casino the required action, try the flat betting method described below.

When you are winning by grinding out units, your trailing stop-loss moves up with your win. For example, assume that you are up a total of twenty-two units (not counting your signing bonus). Your trailing stop-loss of fourteen units would signal stop and withdraw if your winnings drop to eight units, plus your signing bonus.

If you can't detect a choppy game in the casinos' RNG, another approach to exploit the upfront bonus money is to flat bet. Using this approach, you would usually get the money. For example, assume that you deposit $100 and are credited with a $20 signing bonus. You bet $5 a hand playing basic strategy. The casino advantage is less than 1 percent. It would take twenty-four bets to generate the action required to withdraw your money. In a choppy game, you may win twelve and lose twelve. Even if you win eleven and lose thirteen, you've still made 10 percent on your money (not assuming any blackjacks, splits or double downs).

What is the worst that you can do on these twenty-four hands flat betting in the choppy game we have assumed? The worst assumes that the choppy game turns unfavorable and you begin to lose before you decide to get out. Using simple statistics, we can compute the standard deviation on these twenty-four hands as about 2.5 hands. This means that about 68 percent of the time, the worst we could expect is to only win 12 minus 2.5 hands or 9.5 hands and lose 14.5 hands for a net loss of 5 hands or $25. So, overall, you are only down $5. Not a bad risk.

For the above example, if you want to assume two standard deviations, which encompass 95 percent of the probable occurrences, your record for the twenty-four hands could be seven wins and seventeen losses. This losing trend should be respected and the game departed early on using a simple trailing stop-loss technique of three betting units; i.e., anytime you back off three units from a high point, leave the game.

This tactic of hustling signing bonuses is not new. I first learned about it when researching this book in late 1999. Since then, I have communicated with scores of players that are out there using it and taking advantage of the liberal bonuses and action that the hundreds of Internet casinos offer. I first published this strategy in my gambling e-zine (online newsletter), *Advantage Player*, in April 2000.

I know of one example where a gambler hit thirty casinos in one day with max deposits. He played roulette, betting an equal amount on red and black, with a small bet on each zero for insurance. For our $100 deposit example above, betting $12 on red and $12 on black with $1 on each zero, it would take him just five spins to generate the required action. Well, for this particular betting pattern, it didn't take the casinos long to catch on and reprogram their software to detect it and close his account. So I recommend sticking with blackjack and avoiding this kind of hedging at roulette or craps; i.e., betting on both red and black or on the Pass and Don't Pass at craps.

The above example, so easy for the online casinos to detect, poses the question: Is this strategy still valid? The answer is very definitely. Why? Because of the intense competition for players. If a casino dropped the upfront cash bonuses, it would quickly lose players to competing casinos.

With eight hundred casinos to choose from and new casinos opening every week, you can find all the action you can handle.

Theoretically, operating at just two casinos a week, it would take you over eight years to cycle through every casino in cyberspace (in reality you would only be playing at those casinos that are favorably rated).

Can you imagine a real-world casino offering you a 20 percent signing bonus to play blackjack? And then letting you walk out the door with their money after giving them only enough action to equal your buy-in plus their bonus? It seems incredible when you compare the real world with the virtual world. Online casinos can make this offer because they hold your money, have lower overhead expenses, and because they have the odds working their way with the RNG games. So let's take what they give us and turn it into an edge.

Online casinos will continue to make money on this very liberal marketing strategy because most gamblers (unlike the readers of this book) will stay, play, and lose.

There is one catch to this strategy that you need to be aware of and that is getting your money out of the casino. Two recommendations: (1) only play at casinos whose reputations are favorable for releasing players' money; (2) do not stop play and proceed to withdraw on or near the amount of betting action the casino requires before you can take their signing bonus with you; give them enough action so they will think you're a gambler, not a hustler.

Which brings us to Method 3 for generating the desired action.

METHOD 3: DETECTING PATTERNS IN THE CASINO'S PSEUDO RANDOM NUMBER GENERATOR

The feasibility of this method is right at the edge of the state-of-the-art. A few Internet friends and associates are working on such a method. I wanted to mention this to you for two reasons: (1) if you find one or develop one, please contact me and tell me about it; (2) if you are interested in my progress in this arena, please contact me for a progress report.

SUMMARY AND RECOMMENDATIONS

Now let's summarize the three Internet chapters into an integrated strategy:

1. Choose a casino for play, one which offers a 20 to 30 percent signing bonus; stick with Boss Media casinos until you get some experience.

2. Open your account.

3. Use the free-play mode to determine if the casinos' RNG produces a choppy game.

4. If yes, make a deposit and begin play. Insure that the real-money game is exhibiting the same choppy game as the free-play game. Set a stop-loss for this casino and respect it, whether or not you can grab the signing bonus with your withdrawal.

5. If the choppy game is present in the real-money game, use Method 1 to grind out a win using a fourteen-unit trailing stop loss.

6. If no choppy game is present, use a flat betting approach to give the casino the required action before withdrawal.

7. When your fourteen-unit trailing stop-loss is triggered, close your account, withdraw your money, and move to a new casino with another 20 to 30 percent signing bonus.

The key to making this integrated methodology work: Make a plan and stick to it—discipline, discipline, discipline. Review Chapters 3 and 4 before starting play at each new casino to reinforce your objectives.

Twenty-two

PUTTING IT ALL TOGETHER—A SIX-STEP WINNING PROGRAM

In this chapter, I suggest that you focus your energy and adopt the six steps you must follow to become a permanent and consistent winner at casino blackjack. I suggest that you review Chapter 5 after reading this chapter because this chapter picks up from where Chapter 5—mental discipline—left off.

STEP 1: DEVELOP A WINNING ATTITUDE

Believing you can win doesn't mean that you will automatically go to the winning tables and be dealt winning hands. What it does mean is that you will play on *your* terms and not the casinos'. You will play when your level of energy is highest and you can control your emotions. You can develop a winning attitude by practicing the visualization ideas or by using Dr. Steve Heller's Triggers Tactic discussed in Chapter 5. Whatever approach you take, stick with it because it will pay off; not only by increasing your winnings, but also, and more important, by decreasing your losses. Players with winning attitudes know *when* to play—and when *not* to play.

STEP 2: SELECT A WINNING METHOD

This is a key decision, and you should give it your utmost attention. Reading this book and becoming familiar with the strategies and tactics presented will help you to make this decision.

One suggestion: Do not get caught up in the vortex of evaluating card-counting point-count systems. I evaluated eleven of these in the first edition of this book, and there have been at least that many more published in the last decade. My conclusion is the same now as it was then: If you count or decide to learn how to count, use the *High-Low System*. Higher-level point-count systems look good on paper, but they break down under the realities of casino play.

You should think of your card-counting method as only one of a number of tools that you need to win. Remember, this tool applies to only 5 to 10 percent of the hands that you play at the blackjack table.

Another important tool you need is a method for evaluating table biases. Or, at the very least, the recognition that they exist and must be dealt with. I have given you some data in this book to start you out. To learn more about table biases and how to use the twenty-one factors of the Target method for selecting winning tables, consider acquiring the Target/Blackjack Home-Study Course described in Chapter 10. More information on Target 21 can be found in Section 5.

STEP 3: JOIN A SUPPORT GROUP; GET INVOLVED WITH A NETWORK OF WINNERS

Let me give you one of the secrets of becoming a consistent winner: Associate with winners. Get to know winners. Hang around with winners. Their winning attitudes will rub off on you. And you will talk to them, watch them play, practice with them, and find out how they do it. Avoid losers.

You can develop your own support group by getting involved with your friends that play blackjack. Or by teaching them how to play and what winning is all about.

If you are a high roller with a line of credit, the casino may provide your transportation to and from the casino. If they fly you to Atlantic City from New York, for example, you will meet many other gamblers like yourself. Get to know them on the plane and keep an eye on them in the casino. It will be easy to separate the winners from the losers. Associate with the winners and form your support group this way.

What does a support group do? Members exchange information with one another about systems and methods. They talk over problems about why they might have experienced a losing session. They read and discuss the same blackjack books (this one should be tops on their list—recommend it to them and do them a favor).

Support group participants arrange for joint practice sessions and schedule joint trips to the casino. Some even form teams and pool bankrolls or teams to acquire and exchange information about the location of good blackjack tables on the casino floor.

An easy way to get involved with a support group is to take my Blackjack Home Study Course and attend one or more of the follow-up sessions in a casino location. Many blackjack players who attend my follow-up sessions form friendships and support groups that last the rest of their lives.

My blackjack Home Study Courses schedule free update sessions three to four times a year that provide the opportunity to meet and get involved with other players. They also enjoy continuous interaction via an Internet e-mail list server.

STEP 4: DEVELOP A PLAN OF ACTION

It is always surprising to me why so few gamblers develop and document a plan for their blackjack training and their blackjack play. In their careers and everyday business world, they would not think of operating without a plan. Presidents of major corporations have attended my clinics. They spend tens of thousands of dollars in developing yearly operating plans for their companies, but their blackjack activities are run by the seat of their pants with little or no thought given to why they play or what they intend to get out of it.

Start by writing down your goals and objectives. Be as specific as possible. The best articulation of a goal I have ever heard or read was expressed this way: "I intend to win $10,000 a year in part-time play until 1990. At that time I plan to move my family to Las Vegas and become a semiprofessional blackjack player earning $50,000 a year or more." This player knew exactly what he wanted—and he accomplished this goal.

Your plan should include a tentative schedule, and it should definitely include your training activities and the level of skill you intend to achieve. It should include all the methods you intend to utilize, and it should set forth your bankroll and money-management parameters such as betting units, stop-loss, etc.

Your documented plan does not have to be a pretty typewritten piece. In fact, it is better if it is in your own handwriting. When you write something with your own hand, there is a better connection between this physical act and your brain accepting the idea. It is important that you develop the intention to execute your plan and that this intention is nurtured, survives, and becomes real when you take pen or pencil in hand and write down your goals and objectives.

Paraphrasing Winston Churchill's quotation, "This is not the end, but the end of the beginning!" Don't put this book on a shelf—use it! Here is a list of action items and decisions for you to make for your second and subsequent times through this book and for incorporating into this plan of action:

1. Learn Basic Strategy so you can play it automatically. Learn the Clump Card variations and when to apply them.

2. Use the Money Management Work Sheet in Chapter 3 to establish your blackjack bankroll and your betting unit.

3. Use the data in Chapter 5 to develop, document, execute, and evaluate your game plan.

4. Decide from Chapters 20 and 21 whether or not you intend to include the Internet casinos in your game plan.

5. From Chapter 12, decide which blackjack books to acquire and order them.

6. As part of Step 2 leading to this plan of action, decide which winning systems you intend to use and develop a training plan for learning them and implementing them in your home casino area. Consider getting involved with the author's blackjack training program.

7. As part of Step 3 leading to this plan of action, decide on how you intend to join or form a support group. Consider joining the author's network.

8. A plan doesn't mean anything until it's executed. Perhaps it calls for practicing card counting and the Count Profiles Strategy twice a week. The execution is the doing. And you will feel good when you carry out the plan steps.

Execution involves documenting your casino play. You should document every table you play and every session. Your documentation should become a permanent record.

STEP 5: EVALUATE YOUR PROGRESS TOWARD ACCOMPLISHING THE PLAN GOALS AND TAKE CORRECTIVE ACTION AS NECESSARY

This is the most important part of the planning process: evaluation, assessment of progress, definition of problems, and identification of corrective action. A plan is not a static document put on a shelf and referred to once in a while. A plan changes based on feedback from the real world. Steps 4 and 5 are really all part of the planning process: you document your plan, execute it, and evaluate it.

This is why it is important to document every table that you play. This is mandatory if this step is to be successfully accomplished.

STEP 6: GIVE A LITTLE BIT BACK BY HELPING AND WORKING WITH OTHER PLAYERS

There is an amazing phenomenon in the game of blackjack. And that is the synergism that occurs when you work with and help a less experienced player. Your own learning and skills are reinforced, and areas of your own play that need practice and attention are exposed. But better yet is the satisfaction you get by helping the less experienced player. I have been encouraging this with my own students for years and it pays off every time. A wise man once said that you never really learn something until you teach it to someone else. Try it! You really can't understand what I am writing about here until you make it real for yourself.

I execute this Step 6 by writing and updating this book and I will take it a step further right here and extend my personal invitation to you to attend a complimentary blackjack follow-up session. Use the form in the back of this book to request further information and a schedule.

Section Five

PRODUCTS AND SERVICES AVAILABLE FROM JERRY PATTERSON

ABOUT JERRY PATTERSON

Jerry Patterson has a B.A. from Willamette University (1956) and an M.S. from George Washington University (1968). Before becoming a blackjack player, gambling author, and instructor, he spent twenty-five years in the computer systems and services field.

Jerry Patterson has been playing casino blackjack since 1956. He entered the gaming field full-time in 1978 when the Atlantic City casinos opened. He played professional blackjack in the 1980s and managed several blackjack teams during that period. He is the author of five gambling books, all published by The Berkley Publishing Group, a division of Penguin Putnam Inc.

Founded in 1978, his gaming company, Jerry Patterson Enterprises, Inc. (JPE) aka Jerry Patterson's Blackjack Clinic, is the oldest and most successful in the gambling instruction and services field.

Through this company and via his former syndicated casino gaming column published in newspapers and magazines internationally, Patterson has taught millions of gamblers the rudiments and the fine points of how to win at blackjack, craps, and roulette.

Patterson has been involved in researching and developing winning gambling systems since the early 1960s. An example of a notable accomplishment in the blackjack arena is the first Shuffle-tracking method. The initial version was published in 1985 in his book *Break the Dealer*. A final version was published in 1990 in his book *Blackjack: A Winner's Handbook*.

Patterson's research and development activities in casino blackjack started in 1963 when he was working with two of the developers of the original Basic Strategy—Will Cantey and Herb Maisel. With their help, he designed and implemented the first blackjack computer simulation model.

His attention turned to casino roulette and then to casino craps in the 1990s. Much of that work is documented in his book *Casino Gambling*.

About Eric Nielsen

Eric Nielsen is a successful advantage player who has been closely associated with Jerry Patterson since 1990. He spends much of his time researching casino games and developing creative advantage play methodologies.

Eric lectures on casino gaming topics and has successfully led professional blackjack, craps, baccarat, and roulette teams in Las Vegas and Atlantic City. He was the first to develop successful methods to exploit the dealer signature phenomenon in casino roulette. Eric is also expert in the mental discipline aspects of professional play.

Eric developed the Signature Series Roulette program for casino roulette and the Inner Track Guide to Winning mental readiness program for professional players. He coauthored *Casino Gambling* with Jerry Patterson, assisted in the development of the PARR program for casino craps and has authored numerous articles on advantage play topics.

Eric makes his home in south-central Connecticut and can be spotted frequently playing at blackjack, craps, and roulette tables in Atlantic City, Las Vegas, and, closer to his home, at Foxwoods and Mohegan Sun.

THE JERRY PATTERSON CLIENT
NETWORK

In the year 2001, JPE celebrated its 25th year in the gaming instructional business. No other gambling school has been around this long. There are some very important reasons for this longevity that you should know about if you are considering contacting JPE for more information.

The main reason for this longevity is hands-on follow-up support. Patterson and his instructors have always been accessible for their students and clients—by phone, fax, seminars, email, and in the casino. For example, the Target 21 Blackjack Course features free Question and Answer seminars three or four times a year in Las Vegas and Atlantic City. Clients attend as many as they wish and there is never a charge. Some blackjack players have been coming since the beginning in the early 80s. The reason is that these sessions are unstructured Q & As—the attendees set the agenda and, as they tell the instructors, they always learn something new.

Patterson's instructors also check out their students' play in the casino in supervised four- to five-person groups.

The follow-up support wouldn't work, of course, if the methods were not winning methods. JPE has sponsored an ongoing research program since the early 80s in blackjack, since the early 90s in roulette and, since the mid-90s in craps. We keep our systems current and always stay a few jumps ahead of the casinos.

Another reason for Patterson's success is an unconditional refund policy beginning with the first course you buy and extending to any course or service you buy from JPE.

If you do decide to contact Patterson and get involved with one of JPE's home-study courses — available for blackjack, craps, and roulette — you will join a select few. You will network with Patterson's other clients by attending a follow-up seminar or by contact via the Internet. You will enjoy the interaction, the camaraderie, the friendships you will form, and, of course, the winning. The advantage methods at the heart of JPE's gaming instructional programs have been validated and tested by hundreds of man hours; they are proven — they work.

Please keep reading for more details and contact information.

For information about Jerry's bestselling gambling book, *Casino Gambling*, visit his web site: www.CasinoGamblingEdge.com.

THE TARGET 21 INSTRUCTIONAL PROGRAM (SINCE 1985)

Target 21, which stands for Table, Research, Grading & Evaluation Technique, is a method for finding winning tables. We call these tables *player-biased tables* or *dealer-breaking tables*. They result from biases caused by the nonrandom shuffle.

Blackjack Quiz

If you answer "yes" to any of the questions below, you should consider taking advantage of the moneymaking opportunities of the Target 21 Method.

Have you ever sat at a blackjack table where the dealer was breaking a lot and you could do no wrong? You kept beating the dealer hand after hand?

Were you ever $100 or more ahead while playing blackjack but did not leave the table when the cards turned against you? You gave back all your profits and then some?

As a card counter, have you ever lost hand after hand in a very high-count situation with your maximum bet out and seen your trip's profits go down the tubes?

Have you ever won hand after hand with your minimum bet out? How much more would you have made if you could have known the dealer would keep on breaking?

Are you a would-be card counter who practiced at home but could never master counting? Does winning without counting appeal to you?

Have you ever watched a blackjack player making a tremendous amount of money with seemingly little effort? Picture yourself in his or her shoes, taking the money off the table. With Target 21, this is possible.

Characteristics of the Target 21 Method

- Although Target 21 can be played without counting cards, it works well in conjunction with card-counting techniques. But you must use a factor called "table integrity" to decide whether or not to bet up in a high-count situation.

- Card counters enjoy Target 21 because it releases them from the constraints of traditional card-counting techniques. No more searching for those elusive games where you play head-to-head against the dealer; no more playing at odd hours when head-to-head games are supposedly available; no more worries about bad cut-card placement; biases detected by Target 21 transcend the shuffle, so the effect of cut-card placement is reduced. The Target 21 table-entry techniques will get card counters and other blackjack players into many more playable games.

- Target 21 is a short-term moneymaking technique—an important point for today's player. It does not work like traditional card-counting techniques, where many hundreds of play may be required before the mathematics prevail and a player wins money. Through our empirical studies, we have determined that it is possible for Target 21 players to win in up to 70 to 80 percent of their playing sessions, although it is possible, by minimizing table losses and maximizing table wins, to enjoy an overall winning percentage by winning at as few as 40 percent of tables played. Table selection is an investment decision. You expect to win at each and every table that you select. When a table does not offer a return on your investment, we teach you to cut your losses short and make a hasty departure: something like a stop-loss technique that is used in stock market transactions.

- Target 21's short-term advantages make it possible to play with a much smaller bankroll than is required for traditional card-counting techniques. This is because your chances of winning in any given session are much higher. We have experimented with a $100 casino bankroll and watched it appreciate to $500 on many occasions. The $100 was lost less than one time in five.

- Target 21 is a tool that is helpful for high rollers and gamblers even if they do not choose to invest the time to find the player-biased tables. All gamblers need information about when and how much to press their bets no matter at which table they are playing. Target 21 gives them this information and provides them with a winning advantage without counting.

- There are various styles of play associated with the Target 21 Method. Some players scout for biased tables. They use the twenty-one factors to decide whether or not to sit down and play. Others play at a table with only a few of the factors and, as long as they are not losing, wait for the other factors to develop. Some player-biased tables can be detected one or two shoes before the bias kicks in.

- Many Target 21 players adopt the Partner Play style. While one partner plays in a player-biased game, the other scouts for another table in the same casino. If they find a dealer-breaking table, both partners play in the same game.

Questions and Answers about TARGET 21

Why Teach Target 21? Why Not Just Keep It for Yourself?

I have always been an entrepreneur, looking for products that fill a need and then forming businesses to market them. I enjoy teaching and I enjoy showing gamblers how to win. I have owned and operated *The Blackjack Clinic and School of Gambling* since 1977; we make a fair profit, but to be in business this long, we must be doing something right.

Is Target 21 Just for Experienced Players or Professional Players?

No. The twenty-one factors that point to winning tables are easily learned. Many successful Target 21 players visit the casinos just once a month; some only play once or twice a year.

If you learn to play with an edge over the house, you can win. Without training, you have a very good chance of losing on most of your trips. Remember that playing with Basic Strategy is still a losing game. *Disciplined Target 21 players win six to seven trips out of ten.*

What Do the Casinos Do to Stop Target 21 Players From Winning?

If you are a card counter, the casinos can tell if they have someone watching your betting pattern. The betting pattern of a card counter is easily detectable. But with Target 21, there is no way to detect you. You look like an ordinary gambler since you raise your bet when winning and lower it or walk away when losing. Granted, you win more often; but to a pit boss you look like a gambler, so they don't worry.

When the dealer is running cold, the casino could bring in new decks of cards, but this is very time consuming. It aggravates the players and costs the casinos money. They lose money by not dealing during the downtime required to remove the cards from boxes, examine them for marks, "wash" the cards, and perform the new shuffle.

If I Am Already a Card Counter, How Would Target 21 Help My Game?

You use Target 21 to select the tables with a bias in your favor and, after table entry, you start to count. In many cases the count works better at these tables (you do have to verify this, however, by analyzing a Target 21 factor called "Integrity") and you will not have the downswings prevalent in many dealer-biased games.

In many dealer-biased games the count does not work for reasons discussed in this book. For example, the count goes up, but the high cards do not come out as predicted, or they come out in the disadvantageous like-card clumps. The Target 21 course teaches you how to avoid these games.

When Counting, Do I Have to Memorize Cards When I Play? Will It Take the Fun out of the Game?

No. You don't have to memorize cards at all. First of all, you don't have to count when you use Target 21. And, if you do count, all you have to remember is just one number, because each card you see is either added to or subtracted from that running count number.

Playing with Target 21 is fun because you don't have to concentrate if you are not counting. You will enjoy talking to the other players; players at your tables will be more talkative because they are at winning tables that you have selected.

Experiment: On your next trip to the casino, walk around and notice how few people at the blackjack tables look like they are having a good time. You won't see many because most tables are losing tables; and losing is no fun.

How Difficult Is It to Learn?

It is not difficult. The minimum time required is eight to nine hours. It takes that long to go through the audio and video tapes. Target 21 is very logical, which makes it easy to learn and remember. After listening to the audio tapes, watching the video tape, and reading over the course materials, you will know most of the Target 21 factors.

How Many Target 21 Factors Are There?

Twenty-one. If you see six or more, you have a high probability of a winning table. In the Target 21 Home-Study Course, we teach you how to recognize these factors and evaluate them for a table-entry decision. In the early 80s, when we first started using and teaching Target 21, there were just seven factors. Research has continued over the years and confirmed the existence of twenty-one, four of which we call Superfactors because of their extremely strong correlation to winning tables.

When Will Target 21 Be Published in One of Your Books?

The entire method is proprietary and is just too valuable. Target is not a system I ever advertise. The only players who acquire the method are ones who take the time to contact me after reading this or another of my books.

Could I Play Blackjack as a Way of Generating Extra Income?

This is the goal of many of our users. We know they succeed because they come to Update Sessions and we survey them periodically. Others use Target 21 to build a large bankroll so they can enjoy the thrill of betting "green" ($25 chips) or "black" ($100 chips). And still others use their blackjack winnings to finance their trips and vacations to exotic locations.

Can You Describe the Course?

The Target 21 Home-Study Course includes **audio and video tape instruction, training manuals, and telephone and email consultation.** It features in-casino instruction with a small group of students conducted by me or one of my instructors (this is done in such a way that the pit bosses do not know what we are doing). In addition, Target 21 Update and Q & A seminars are offered periodically in casino cities.

Target 21 is a unique instructional program and your inquiries are invited. Please email or call my office **toll free** for a **free twelve-page brochure** or use the coupon at the back of this section to request one. An outline of the course follows.

Target 21 Course Outline

Lesson 1: Understanding Target 21 and Why You Win

- How to Select a Moneymaking Table
- How One Target 21 Superfactor Can Almost Guarantee Your Profits
- When to Leave the Table with Profits in Hand
- How and Why Target 21 Solves the Problems Associated with Card Counting
- How to Use Target 21 to Pick Tables Where the Count Really Works
- Definitions of Bias and Nonrandom Shuffles and How They Work to Your Advantage
- Why the "Wash" Makes Certain Games Off-Limits
- Understanding the Different Types of Shuffles and How They Work to Your Advantage or Disadvantage
- Special Drills for Target 21 Casino Practice

Lesson 2: Exploiting Target 21's Profit Potential

- Questions and Answers from a Live Target 21 Classroom Session
- How to Increase Your Profits by Using a Disciplined Documentation Method
- Money Management: Flat Betting (Betting the Same Amount) and When to Use It
- Money Management: When to Bet and When Not to Bet with the Count

- Money Management: Special Techniques for Recreational Gamblers, High Rollers, and Junket Players

- Tips for Creating the "Home Run Tables" Where the Dealer Breaks Hand After Hand

- How to "Tune" Your Play to Exploit the Special Advantages in the Atlantic City Game or which can be found in other casino locations such as Foxwoods or the many Mississippi locations

- Nuances for the Variety of Games in Nevada

- "Action Target": Amazing Moneymaking Opportunities for Nevada's Single-Deck Games

- When and How to Avoid Losing by Standing on Stiff Hands

- How to Evaluate a Casino for Target 21 Play

Lesson 3: Casino Session
How the Casino Session Works:

- Instructor Selects Target 21 Tables for Review and Comment

- Students Practice Scouting and Table Selection with Instructor Feedback (away from the casino floor)

- Instructor Monitors Table Departure

Target 21 course materials

(1) six hours of audio cassette tapes, (2) two hours of videotape, (3) a comprehensive training manual, (4) a portfolio of expanded Target course materials and follow-up support: access to Target hotline; telephone, and email consultation with Jerry Patterson and his instructors; and Target 21 Update seminars in Atlantic City, Las Vegas, Reno/Tahoe, and other major locations — all at no additional cost — ever.

Call TOLL-FREE 1-800-257-7130 or email jpe21@aol.com and ask for a free twelve-page brochure, which describes the Target Method. Or send us the Information Request Coupon at the back of this chapter.

Please note that if you decide to order this unique instructional program, you take absolutely no risk because you are protected by an unconditional and legally binding guarantee.

THE BLACKJACK MASTERS PROGRAM (SINCE 1996)

The Blackjack Masters Program is an Advanced Blackjack Course available to graduates of the Target 21 Course.

Here are just a few of the advanced techniques you will learn:

- How to anticipate player-favorable rounds and bet up into them; a higher percentage of big bets won yields a higher table win rate, more winning sessions and more dollars per hour of play;

- How to anticipate dealer-favorable rounds and reduce the bet to table minimum to keep your losses low and not eat into the profits you've already accumulated in this game;

- How to read the dealer's hole card; really! Not every time, mind you, but often enough to give you a tremendous feeling of power. Visualize yourself at third base, predicting a low hole card under the ten up, standing on a stiff hand and watching the dealer break.

- How to predict whether or not the next card out of the shoe will be high or low; how many times have you doubled down on an eleven only to see the dreaded low card come out of the shoe? Now you'll have a much better chance of doubling into a high card because you'll be predicting them!

- How to find and exploit biased shoes, either hand- or machine-shuffled, with the powerful Killer Progression

- How to forecast whether or not the next shoe will be favorable. How many times have you left a table and wondered about that next shoe? Now you'll have the ability, based on game reading, to stay into a profitable shoe, or leave and avoid that losing shoe.

THE SHARPSHOOTER CRAPS HOME-STUDY AND IN-CASINO TRAINING PROGRAM (SINCE 1996)

For casino craps, we teach you how to create your own edge over the casino by setting and controlling the dice to avoid the losing seven after the winning point number has been established. The advantage method and home study course is called Sharpshooter Craps.

The course consists of videotape and audiotape instruction combined with a seventy-page instruction manual and supervised dealer-school practice sessions and monitored in-casino play.

The instruction is aimed at learning and applying the five linch-pins: (1) The Set; (2) The Grip; (3) The Focus; (4) The Controlled Throw, or Rhythm Roll, and (5) The bet.

Betting and Money-Management Methods are also included. Feel free to request a descriptive brochure.

For full details about this popular course for achieving and advantage over the casinos, visit Jerry's web site: CasinoGambling-Edge.com. Click dice control.

THE SIGNATURE SERIES ROULETTE HOME-STUDY COURSE (SINCE 1994)

The Signature Series course teaches you how to detect and qualify the dealer signature in many games with the use of a quick, simple "charting" procedure. Players exploit the signature with an advantage over the casinos by placing bets on five inside numbers, "straight up." Players exploit their advantage by using either a conservative flat-betting approach, which can yield substantial units per hour of profit, depending on skill level and casino conditions; for example, the number of spins per hour is dependent on the number of players in the game, or on one of several aggressive up-as-you-win approaches, which can multiply the hourly profit derived by flat-betting!

One of the most attractive features of the Signature Series methods is that no large bankrolls are required. Players can begin with a bankroll of no more than $250. In casino locations that offer low-stakes games, a starting bankroll of only $60 or $70 is adequate.

Signature Series methods are unique—like nothing you have seen before. They have nothing to do with the mechanically biased wheels, biased sectors, or extended up-as-you-lose betting schemes. The methods are completely legal and involve no cheating or use of hidden electronic equipment. They are quick and simple and can be effectively employed even in the fastest of game conditions.

The instructional program is an easy-to-follow home study format. It consists of an easy-to-understand manual, two audiotape supplements, and a series of "practice pack" exercises, complete with a regulation-size table layout felt and a supply of casino-quality chips for home practice. In-casino signature identification and validation are part of the program.

You are invited to request complete details.

Information Request Form to contact Jerry Patterson

BY PHONE: (800) 257-7130 OR (775) 265-9224
OR TEAR THIS PAGE OUT AND FAX TO: (775) 265-0085
EMAIL: *jpe21@aol.com*
WEB SITE: www.casinogamblingedge.com
OR SEND THIS FORM TO:
Jerry Patterson Enterprises, Inc.
P.O. Box 236
Gardnerville, NV 89410-0236

Dear Jerry,

I want more information about becoming an Advantage Player and overcoming the casino edge; please send detailed information on your systems, methods, and home-study courses I have checked below:

[ ] Blackjack/TARGET 21 Home-Study Course to find winning tables where the shuffle bias favors the player for overcoming the house edge
[ ] Blackjack Masters Advanced Study Program
[ ] Sharpshooter Craps Home-Study Course for developing a controlled throw and overcoming the house edge
[ ] Signature Series Home-Study Course for casino roulette for detecting and exploiting dealer signatures and overcoming the house edge

Also send me the free information I have checked below:

[ ] Update Report on Internet casinos and gambling-oriented web sites
[ ] Wallet-size blackjack Basic Strategy cards
[ ] Enclosed is $13.95, plus $4.00 S&H, a total of $17.95. Send Jerry's bestselling gambling book, *Casino Gambling*.

[ ] Please send information about updates or other items noted in this book; specifically I am interested in the following: _____

_____

Name: _____

Street Address: _____

City/State/Zip: _____

E-mail address (optional): _____